LOVE IS BANANAS

Crystal!

LOVE IS BANANAS

ONE MAN'S JOURNEY TO
DISCOVER THE MOST IMPORTANT
WORD IN THE WORLD

*This is a Book
I swear to God.*

Love

TREY HUMPHREYS

Trey

NEW DEGREE PRESS

COPYRIGHT © 2020 TREY HUMPHREYS

LOVE IS BANANAS

One Man's Journey to Discover the Most Important Word in the World

ISBN

978-1-63676-640-9   *Paperback*

978-1-63676-187-9   *Kindle Ebook*

978-1-63676-192-3   *Digital Ebook*

I dedicate this book to myself. I did it.

CONTENTS

———

Your task is not to seek for love, but merely to seek and find all the barriers within yourself that you have built against it

—RUMI

And if you have the ability to love, love yourself first

—CHARLES BUKOWSKI

AUTHOR'S NOTE

———

"I am seeing you at a typewriter," Beverly anxiously blurted out thirty-two seconds into our video call. She was in Los Angeles, and I was sitting on a park bench five thousand miles away. For the next thirty minutes she meandered through a variety of topics, including a primal witch doctor, archangels, a lotus flower, sun activations, and muckraking in the 1930s. A friend had gifted me a psychic session with her.

She finally took a breath and asked, "Are you in the process of creating something new or writing something?"

"Yeah, a book about love."

Love is the most complicated, painful, confusing, wonderful, goofy, complex, and mystical thing I have ever tried to understand. So was my session with Beverly.

I never planned on writing this book. Hell, I never planned on writing a book, period. I can barely spell and had failed English in high school. I also never planned on being forty-seven years old, single, and still trying to figure out love. So, let's get on with it.

I decided to write this book because I was tired of all the boring self-help books, looney therapists, and bachelor TV shows that make a disaster out of love. I was tired of Disney movies promising us "happily ever after" once we met our "perfect soulmates" and fell "in love at first sight." I was tired of not being good at love.

My journey started a few years ago with one simple question from a business coach.

What is your definition of love?

It blindsided me. My answer was awful.

Since then I have searched the world over for the answers to love. From the backseat of a Toyota truck in Yemen, where I heard a beautiful love story from a broken man, to a snake-handling preacher in Kentucky. I sat in a dirty motel room with a twenty-eight-year-old homeless girl who was HIV positive and riddled with cancer. Then I spent time with Ralph, who was 101 years old. Through it all I have asked everyone I met the same three questions:

1. What's your definition of love?
2. How many times have you been in love?
3. Do you love yourself?

My hope is you find love in these pages and let it become contagious in your life. I actually think it's pretty simple, and through my travels around the world and the people I have met, I've found love is right in front of us. It's always right in front of us if we just open our eyes.

You are going to LOVE this book if you are tired of eating pizza alone on Friday nights, sick of self-help books, and want to step up your love game. This book is for anyone who has ever been in love, wants to find love, or needs to rediscover self-love. Over the next thirty-three chapters we will laugh together, cry together, and love together.

At the end of my session with Beverly the psychic, she said the following words about this book:

"I bless this book in the spirit of unconditional love. May all benefit from this authentic tale and be drawn to it and read it with great fervor and passion. May everyone really experience this spiritual enlightenment. Let this book be in the vibration of love."

Amen, girl, amen.

Trey

1

LOVE IS BANANAS

1

WHAT IS LOVE?

———

Love is confusing, elusive, cheesy, questionable, and mysterious. It can make the hair stand up on your neck and slap you in the face. It's a force beyond comprehension and the oxygen for our souls. We want it. We need it. We love it. So how do we do it? Well, from the oddballs I have talked to and the crazy places I have been, it all starts with loving ourselves. In this part of the book you get a sneak peek into the disaster which was my life, as well as a few unique folks I have met along the way. Buckle up, it's a bumpy ride.

2

A SINGLE QUESTION

———

"Bananas are harder on the outside to protect them from the mushy stuff inside, like people. Love is mushy."

– PAYTON, ELEVEN YEARS OLD

He stared at me. I stared at him. I sat lifeless in a small chair surrounded by whiteboards. I was hoping he was my last hope.

The thing about rock bottom is it's hard. Rocks are hard. I found rock bottom. My personal life was miserable; I was single, broke, and hopeless. My business life wasn't much better. I had started several businesses over the years that were flat or losing money. I was also aging and god, aging sucks. It was four days before my fortieth birthday. I didn't have a girlfriend, dog, cat, or plant. My refrigerator was empty, and I was still using the same bedding from college. All my previous relationships ended with me calling them quits.

Most rational people hire a therapist when life gets out of whack. I was too proud for that. I hired a business coach instead.

Jimmy, the red-headed business coach, had been digging in my brain for two hours. He was a high-end executive coach with more energy than the sun. I was a mess. In general, it takes me a minute to trust someone. Especially someone digging in my brain. I had started a party bus company with buses covered in fake fur, an event company that threw costume parties, bought the oldest dive bar in the area, and opened a new restaurant. The coach was trying to figure out how to bring them all back to life. What he didn't realize was it was me who needed to be brought back to life. On the outside, I looked successful. On the inside, I was a disaster.

My love life was as dry as the moon, and my friendships were surface-level at best. And I mean at best. I avoided all networking of any kind and hated sales because they involved talking to humans. My entire life could be summarized as hiding behind a mask, a bar, a DJ booth, or a joke to make sure nobody saw the real me.

I debated for weeks about hiring a coach. It was not cheap but I was cheap. Eventually I broke and signed up for a session.

I arrived at his house, took a <u>deep</u> breath, and knocked on the door. He opened with a 'let's fix your life' smile. He had arranged a war room full of business-type things like whiteboards, large paper pads, and markers. He had been a high-level executive in a Fortune 500 company on the fast track to becoming CEO until he said, 'screw it' and started a successful coaching business. I didn't feel like I belonged in the room with him. I can barely spell and ran a business with furry buses, among other things.

He bounced around the room asking question after question while trying to figure out what was wrong. He was wearing Nike running shoes, a golf shirt, jeans, and a smile. I sat lifeless in a chair, staring at the whiteboards as my anxiety grew to unheard levels. After two hours he seemed deflated. I could tell he was perplexed. He scratched his head and asked, "Why don't we take a break?"

"Sure," I said, relieved to stop talking about my miserable businesses.

"I am going to grab a coffee in the other room. Why don't you just write your definition of love on the board while I grab the coffee?" he asked as he walked out of the room.

Easy enough, I thought. I stared at the whiteboard. Then I wrote my definition of love on the board. After I wrote it, I took a step back and read what I wrote.

Whoa.

Jimmy returned to the room and looked at the board. I could see the blood drain out of his face and his forehead creased.

His voice softened. "Well, I guess we should start there..."

There were five words on the board.

Love is a painful hell.

When I wrote those words, everything in my entire life made sense to me. The failing businesses, the surface-level friendships, and the lack of intimate relationships. I realized in that moment I truly believed love was hell. I had been disappointed so many times when I was younger I now associated love with pain and avoided it at all costs. This belief kept me from developing healthy relationships in my life. It kept me from engaging with people. It kept me hiding behind my walls, masks, and businesses. I was a lonely man hiding from the world.

And so, my journey began. I had to figure out love and change my life.

A single question from a red-headed business coach altered my entire life. It also taught me one of the most important lessons in life and love.

Ask for help.

Since then, I have been on a journey to discover love. I believe love is the only thing that matters. It is my North Star. A friend once told me if you want to master anything, you have to put in the hours. I want to master love. It will be the hardest thing I have ever done in my life. It has taken me all over the world and into the depths of my soul. I hope together, through the following stories, we can both be a little better at love. If so, we can have everything we want in life.

LOVE LESSONS

1. Master vulnerability - Asking for help requires vulnerability. It requires us to allow others to see inside where the mess is. It requires us to be okay while not being okay and being okay telling someone we are not okay. Okay?

2. Show up - Asking for help requires us to show up when we don't want to show up. To actually sit with another human being and feel feelings. To show up and connect with each other. Connect as in, how are you really doing?

3. Find a banana - You need someone in your corner: coach, therapist, mentor, friend, or sibling. Find one and create a cadence of contact preferably once a week. Find someone who can support you during both the good times and the bad. Practice being vulnerable with them. Don't partner with a pessimist, negative Nancy, heroin addict, or cult leader. Choose a friend, therapist, mentor, or coach who you respect. Start a weekly check-in at the same time and same day each week.

3

MY FAKE FATHER

———

"Bananas are healthy and good for your heart, just like love."
— KAILEY, SIXTEEN YEARS OLD

We were all sitting on the floor. I was near the back. It was the second day of a weekend-long retreat. I was not having a good time.

"Trey?" the leader said, pointing at me from the center of the room. Her eyes burned a hole in my soul. It was my turn.

She was a tiny woman with black hair and dark skin. There wasn't an ounce of fat on her. Her clothing was dark, hiding her small frame. All weekend she drank a bright yellow drink. I got a creepy feeling when she looked at me. No smile. No jokes. No softness in her face. Goosebumps sprang up on my arms and begged me to run out of the building. Her eyes were glued to mine as she called me to the center of the room.

I stood up slowly and made my way to her. Forty people were scattered around the room, but only seventeen were participants like me. The others, I learned, had been through the program before and were now 'angels' there to guide us. Seventeen of us were the broken ones. I reached her and took a deep breath.

My journey to figure out love has been a doozy. What began as a simple question from a red-headed business coach has turned into a lifelong mission. Where does one look when seeking profound answers to the greatest mystery of all time—love? Google, of course. Well, that and therapy, I guess. However, therapists make me squirmy. I once made a therapist cry in a session where I was the client. I started talking about how I loved my mom and looked up to see tears running down her face. When I saw her crying, I asked if she was okay. Then I realized I had just asked a therapist in a therapy session if she was okay. Mind bender.

A friend of mine, who had overcome a disastrous season of life during her twenties, suggested I attend this weekend retreat. She said it was a powerful experience. When I looked it up online, the website had words like "awareness" and "heart-centered" and "sacred" and "spirit." Sounded weird. I signed up.

"What's wrong?" the tiny woman asked once I got to the center of the room.

"I don't know," I replied. I really didn't know. Her eyes were dark and my legs were shaking.

Two assistants stood beside her. They donned the usual draperies of spiritualists: long, flowing clothing and crystal necklaces. The rest of the people in the room were sitting on the floor staring at me. My stomach was churning. My mind was going berserk. My soul wanted to call an Uber.

"Your mom?" She stepped closer.

"Maybe," I replied, clueless if that was the case.

"Nope," she said immediately, as if she could sense my entire life history in the blink of an eye.

"Your dad?" Her head tilted.

"Maybe," I replied, clueless if that was the case.

"Yes. It's your dad," she said, staring me directly in the eye without a single hint of emotion on her face. "Pick someone in the room that looks like your dad."

Shit.

The tiny woman read my body language as she asked me questions. She claimed the body doesn't lie. She had a magical ability to know all of your darkest demons without you knowing all of your darkest demons. A total freak.

What I was about to experience was called Gestalt Therapy. *Psychology Today* describes Gestalt Therapy as, "instead of simply talking about past situations, clients are encouraged to experience them, perhaps through reenactment."[1]

It was about to get ugly.

I chose a man that looked like my dad. He was an older guy in his late sixties with a beard and glasses. A kind looking man. She had him stand directly in front of me. We were a foot apart. The rest of the people stood up and gathered around us, making a tightly closed circle. My fake dad and I stood facing each other. The tiny woman stood glued beside us. My heart raced.

The tiny woman whispered in my ear and told me exactly what to say to my pretend father. I was instructed to keep looking him in the eyes. She then whispered in his ear what to say back to me. She created the entire conversation. A very hard conversation.

I fought tears as they welled up in my eyes. I hate crying in front of people. When I was young, I decided to quit feeling feelings. I had been hurt so many times I never wanted anyone to see me cry again. Well, that was about to change.

She leaned over and whispered in my ear, "Dad, you hurt me. You let me down. You broke my heart."

---

1   "Gestalt Therapy," Psychology Today, accessed Aug 10, 2020.

So I repeated it to my fake dad keeping eye contact. A lightning bolt of fear shot through my body. Tears exploded from my eyes.

"I am sorry, son. I am sorry I was not a good father to you. I love you," my fake father said back to me, taking direction from the tiny woman. His bottom lip shaking.

"I hate you, Dad, I hate you!" I screamed a lifetime's worth of pain at the poor man across from me. He started to cry but stood tall, playing the part.

The tiny woman kept feeding us lines to say to each other. My entire body was rattling. I could barely breathe through the screams and tears.

My father was an alcoholic my entire life. He was also my hero. A hero who missed birthdays and showed up to soccer games drunk. A man I idolized and hated at the same time. I always looked up to him. He destroyed me. Then he died in a motel room, alone, when I was twenty-one years old.

I can't remember exactly what I was screaming but at one point I simply broke. My knees buckled, and my legs gave out. I collapsed. The people around me had to hold me up. I couldn't feel my legs. My arms were limp.

The group screamed with me. One big wave of rage pointed at a dead man. I went to a dark place I had never experienced before. The man across from me had a river of tears running down his face.

Then the truth came out…

"I just want to be loved!" I screamed, over and over. A guttural cry for love burst out of me like hell fire.

"Hug your father," the tiny woman finally instructed.

We hugged, and the group settled back onto the floor. My legs started working again, and I caught my breath. I squeezed the man like a drowning child clinging to a lifeguard.

The rest of the weekend was a blur. It included eye-gazing exercises, guided meditations with dolphins, and more Gestalts. I finished the weekend completely drained.

I didn't realize what was missing until that weekend and that conversation with my fake father. Looking back, I could see what a powerful influence my father had been in my life and how desperately I craved his love. How desperately I craved love in general.

In the article "Why Do We Fall in Love?" Psychologist Dr. Beverly Palmer suggests what children learn about love from their parents determines how they will love others as adults. She says, "If your parents fulfilled your need to be emotionally nurtured by giving you love, you then develop into an adult who has love to give. But if your emotional needs were not nurtured, you did not fully develop and instead became a demanding and anxious adult still seeking the love you missed as a child."[2]

I was seeking love. In some way, I think we all are. I realized I had a lot more work to do after that weekend. I also realized how much pain my father caused me over the course of my life. Especially the one time he destroyed me...

LOVE LESSONS

1. We all just want to be loved. Period. Sometimes our parents do a great job loving us. Sometimes they don't. If not, we have to teach ourselves love by going to experiences like this one. It was not fun, but it put a crack in my walls and taught me how much I desperately wanted to be loved.

---

2   Alia Hoyt, "Why Do We Fall in Love," How Stuff Works, February 8, 2018.

2. Finding a group of people to support you is hard because you have to get out of your comfort zone. However, it is a very important part of the process and can teach us how to love as adults.

3. Invest in yourself. Go to a retreat, therapeutic experience, horse therapy, psychiatrist, dude ranch, yoga class, tribal African dance, whatever. You know what you need, now go ask for help. Spend money.

4

MY REAL FATHER

"Bananas love each other...that's why they hug when they are in a bunch."

– ZOE, SEVEN YEARS OLD

I stood in the foyer of my grandmother's small house. My dad stood before me in a robe and white underwear. His eyes were hollow. He was slumped over. It was three o'clock in the afternoon.

Dad had been on a bender for two days. Most of the time he stayed in the guest bedroom of my grandmother's house. He had been living with her, off and on, for the majority of my childhood. I don't think he had a job my entire life. Pathetic.

Dad fell in love with the bottle around the time I was born. He was a godlike figure to me as he popped in and out of my life. I wanted to be like him; funny, smart, and strong. He had one of those personalities that drew everybody in. Charming. Prior to the booze he was wildly successful, owning Rolls-Royce cars and partying all over the world.

Drunk Dad was different. He turned into a soulless shell of a man. A dark, confusing, evil figure to me. I wanted to hide when this dad was around. Not be seen. Disappear. Most of the time, I couldn't.

Whenever my dad asked me to do something, I complied. I am not sure if it was because he was powerful and I was a pansy or if it was easier to shut up than engage with him. I loved him with all my heart and hated him with the rest.

As I stood before him in my grandmother's foyer, he told me to go to his room. His room was small, dark, and miserable, with a broken mattress and a thousand cigarette butts in a silver Rolls-Royce ashtray next to the bed. It reeked of desperation and darkness. I'd finally had enough.

"No," I said to him for the first time in my life.

No to all the bullshit and pain I had been experiencing my whole life. No to being his doormat. No to letting him control me when he was wasted. I finally stood up for myself, and it felt amazing.

Then he attacked me.

He grabbed my arm and twisted it behind my back. He squeezed the breath out of me. I froze in shock. Paralyzed. A moment later my grandmother turned the corner and saw him attacking me. Our eyes connected and I felt all the fire in hell pour out of her as she unleashed a guttural scream. I thought she was going to murder him.

My father let go immediately. I turned and ran out of the house. I ran through yard after yard until I couldn't breathe. Finally, I collapsed against a brick wall and cried a lifetime of tears. Completely destroyed.

I have carried the pain of that moment my entire life. A deep-rooted fear if I stand up for myself, I won't be loved. A fear if I rock the boat, people won't love me. A fear love is pain.

It would take another thirty years for me to rewrite the story of that afternoon. On my birthday, thirty years later, I would finally understand what really happened and found something I'd been missing my whole life...

LOVE LESSONS

1. Sometimes we do not recognize the massive impact experiences from our childhood have on us. Experiences that shape our beliefs on love, life, and ourselves.

2. My grandmother was my rock. Everybody needs a rock. Even if just one rock. Find your rock and be a rock for someone.

3. If your father attacks you, don't run. Turn around and beat his ass.

5

THE GIANT MAN

—

"Bananas are like love because you have to peel them to get to the good stuff which takes work, and that is like love...it takes a lot of work too."

— JAKE, EIGHT YEARS OLD

I never wanted to go. It would be too embarrassing. People would think I was a loser. And pathetic.

Because of the lack of childhood affection I received from my father, I squeaked by without having to face love for most of my life. Sure, I had a few girlfriends and a handful of odd pets, but I never loved deeply. I built imaginary walls to keep love out. I decided to hell with everybody else, I was done caring. Nobody would break my heart again. And so, all my relationships were surface-level, I always broke them up first, and I guarded my heart at all costs. I had no idea what I was really missing. Until...

A giant broke me.

I was working in my office in Atlanta one day and saw a Facebook ad for an upcoming event in California. It was a four-day experience with the giant.

I had always been fascinated by the giant but never had the balls to go see him. Partly because I was too broke to pay for it and partly because I thought only losers go to his events. I noticed the event started on my birthday. Hmm…a sign from the universe or a nudge from the devil? It was being held in Los Angeles which meant I could invite myself to stay with a friend for free. I decided to go just to see the giant perform. Worst case, it would be a hell of a show, I thought. Best case, I might figure out my life. No pressure.

I snuck off to California and slipped into the event Thursday around noon. It was being held in a basketball arena on the campus of a local college. There were nine thousand people. I grabbed a seat in the nosebleeds to hide. The guy next to me was from Central Africa and looked confused. He fidgeted with the program, flipping from page to page and looking up occasionally. He was wearing a nice suit at an event that did not necessitate a nice suit. Middle-aged women in bedazzled sweatpants, young people in horrible sneakers, and worn-down middle age men desperate for the secrets of life filled row after row. I wondered if my new African neighbor had any idea what was about to happen. My guess was no. Neither did I.

Around two in the afternoon, the stage came alive. The arena went dark as dance lights blasted across the crowd. High-energy music pumped through massive speakers as cheerleaders took the stage. Then the giant appeared…

Tony Robbins.

If you don't know who Tony Robbins is, well, he is, in my opinion, the greatest human being alive. You might remember him from his trillion infomercials back in the day that ran ALL THE DAMN TIME. He would flash his big teeth and promise to fix your life. Everybody bought his motivational tapes in the 80s and 90s and now he owns a plane and all the money on earth. He bought a castle in his twenties, built a resort in Fiji in his thirties, and now runs the world. He has been helping people for forty years. I don't think he has slept yet.

Tony was once a sad night janitor from a broken family with nowhere to go. Growing up, he dealt with his mother's mental illness as multiple men came in and out of his life. After he hit rock bottom early in life, he decided to change his story. Now his passion is to help others change their stories. And he is very fucking good at it.

He bolted onto stage wearing black pants and a black shirt. The place went bananas. The man is enormous. The African guy next to me was frozen with eyes the size of dinner plates. I think I saw his heart leave his body and call a taxi.

Tony was damn near seven feet tall, built like an ox, and shaped like a giraffe. He clapped his hands like a broken sewing machine. Jam, jam, jam. You could see his teeth from outer space. I was mesmerized.

Immediately, he had everybody high-fiving and hugging each other. The African guy next to me awkwardly high fived me as if nobody had ever taught him how. I already wanted to put him in my pocket, tell him everything was going to be okay, and protect him from all the madness. I was getting nervous myself. Joyfully hugging strangers is about as fun as sleeping in cold mud. Awkward and uncomfortable. Plus, I am an introvert who prefers to avoid human beings in general. Welcome to hell.

For the next twelve hours, Tony commanded the stage. I didn't see him leave the stage once. There were no breaks in the program. Just a gigantic man talking, clapping, screaming, and pacing for twelve hours. He has to be an alien.

The next two days were exhausting. Stand up, sit down, hug, clap, high five.

Then it happened on Saturday night.

We had been going all day. I was zapped. You get that way at a seminar that serves "fix your life" through a fire hose. If I had to high five one more...

"The next part of the program is going to be very intense. I suggest all young people leave during this part of the program," Tony explained to the audience from the stage.

What?

A pudgy, young volunteer stood in the aisle next to me and said, "This is the best part." His smile told me we were all about to die.

Next, Tony guided us through a hypnotic visualization exercise about our lives. For a little over an hour, he led us through a doomsday visualization about what our lives would be like in the future if nothing changed. It was horrific. I pictured myself dying in a motel room just like my dad. Alone. In pain. Looking back on a wasted life. A life where I failed to love and be loved. A life where I never came close to my potential.

Sad music played in the background as Tony kept pushing us to see our future, feel our future, and feel the potential failure. People were losing their minds. Screams could be heard around the arena. It was beyond eerie as I stood in the dark visualizing and stepping into the worst version of my future. Tears rolled down my face. My heart ached. I felt miserable. It was working.

Then the music changed. So did Tony. He started building us up with new affirmations. Messages of love and hope. Messages of triumph. The ol' 'you can do it' kind of stuff. Then it happened.

Tony's voice was rattling the rafters. The music had grown to a roar. My heart was racing and my body was vibrating. I stood in the aisle with my arms raised and tears flowing down my face. My eyes were closed, and a massive smile paralyzed my face. As instructed by Tony, I stepped into an imaginary beam of yellow light.

Then, in an instant, I felt it. An acceptance I had never experienced before. A total love for myself.

I never knew what it meant to "love yourself." The phrase has never made any sense to me. However, in that moment when I stepped into the imaginary yellow light, I felt it. It was the most powerful moment of my entire life. I felt an authentic, real love for myself. It felt like a thousand pounds of hell fell off my shoulders. A lifetime of doubt, insecurity, pain, and sadness evaporated out of my body. Tears of joy flooded my face. I wasn't embarrassed, shy, or concerned about anything else in the world. I was alive, truly alive.

Self-love is a funny thing. It could be the most important force in the world. The foundation for all love. I never realized how the lack of love for myself kept me from accepting love from others. How the lack of love for myself kept me from giving love to others. I have realized we cannot give what we do not have. It is simple math. Self-love is the foundation of a healthy, happy life. I decided in that moment, in that arena, my mission in life would be to fully understand and step into love.

So as I set out to figure out love, I have asked everyone I've met if they love themselves. I am afraid to say over 80 percent say no. The new question now is if we don't, how do we learn to love ourselves?

Elizabeth, a twenty-eight-year-old homeless girl, provided some insight about self-love. She also broke my heart...

LOVE LESSONS

1. Self-love is the first step toward understanding, accepting, and giving love. Until we love ourselves, we will never be healthy enough to love others fully. We will never have the capacity to accept love from others.

2. Rumi said what you seek is seeking you. The stars lined up and I attended an experience that helped heal my heart. Buy yourself an experience for your next birthday. Experiences change us.

3. Go to a Tony Robbins event before it is too late and his time has passed. It is the greatest show on earth.

6

THE HOMELESS GIRL

———

"A banana may have a bruise but you still eat it and it is delicious, and if you love someone they may have bruises too but you still should love them."

– ALEX, NINE YEARS OLD

I found her on Facebook. She was in a picture holding an ugly lizard. Huge smile. Possibly Mexican. Possibly not. Her, not the lizard.

A homeless girl in Nashville. The Facebook post was from a guy who found her in a park and raised money to get her a motel room. My friend Ilene, who I have known for several years and has the innate ability to find anything on earth, found her. Of course. Ilene loves finding things on the Internet. Like a ferret. So, Ilene asked the girl if I could interview her. The girl said yes.

"Nice!" I shrieked when Ilene told me she would meet with us. "We have to go tomorrow!"

"Tomorrow?" Ilene cringed.

The next day Ilene and I drove to Nashville. I had to meet this girl.

"Do you like Coca-Cola?" was the text Ilene received as we drove up from Atlanta. "I can walk to the store and buy you something to drink," said Elizabeth, the twenty-eight-year-old homeless girl.

We arrived after dark and stopped at a coffee shop where I jotted down thirty-three questions to ask her. While I was working on them, Elizabeth called Ilene and told her that Ty Ty, a drunk homeless woman, would be passed out on the bed. Danny, a homeless man, would be there but would leave us alone. She said they were her "street parents." She also said she was an alcoholic but never gets out of control. Things were shaping up horrifically.

Strange people lingered around outside the motel when we arrived. It was dark. My nerves on high alert. Shady suspects with curious eyes lingered around the hotel. The low-budget motel on the outskirts of Nashville was worn down and dim. Ilene was unfazed. She is fearless.

We found Elizabeth's room. I knocked on the door and took a deep breath. I was not well-versed in hanging out with homeless women in hotel rooms.

She opened and immediately shut the door in my face. Wonderful.

She opened the door again with a huge smile. She had caramel skin and beaming brown eyes. I was shocked at how physically fit she looked. I wasn't expecting her to be pretty, but she was. She wore a pair of sweatpants, a tank top shirt, and high top tennis shoes. I hugged her to try and break the ice. The homeless guy in the corner stared at us with a broken face. A lump of a woman laid motionless on the bed. The room was the size of a closet. It smelled like old carpet and hopelessness.

We sat down at a rickety table in the corner of the room next to the bed. A huge vodka bottle sat in the center of the table. She took a swig straight from the bottle and started telling us her story. I needed a swig.

Every other word out of her mouth was "all the way." Her accent sounded slightly Jamaican and British, but she was half-Mexican and half-something else.

Elizabeth was born in Indiana and was adopted when she was five weeks old. She has five siblings. Her oldest brother is a priest, and her oldest sister is a missionary. The next sister is in the Peace Corps. One of her younger brothers is autistic, and her other brother is gay. That is a well-rounded family.

She found it difficult to be non-white in a Catholic high school. She competed in track and field and won awards. She started her own marketing company at the age of sixteen, loves to sing, and writes her own music. She loved her grandmother but won't talk about the rest of her family. She said almost nothing about her parents.

The man in Nashville who posted her on Facebook found her sleeping in the park. She has colon cancer, throat cancer, skin cancer, and is HIV positive. She is an alcoholic and suffers from seizures. The manic depression doesn't bother her too much, she claims. She has overdosed six times and been to rehab or detox twenty-three times. She has been engaged three times and been abused all three times. One caused her to lose her baby, one knocked a tooth out, and the other infected her with HIV, drugged her, and locked her in a van for six months.

She doesn't like to cry and was very matter of fact when describing the horrific events she has survived. It seemed as if she detached from the stories as she told them to me.

After high school, she tried to focus on her music and moved around, spending time in California and Minnesota. She took a vacation to Detroit and met a man whose mother had recently passed away. He asked her if she would give him a ride to see his deceased mother's funeral. Instead, he drugged her and took her to a gang initiation. She was the bait. She would not talk about what happened but said the drug paralyzed her body but not her mind. She remembers everything that happened to her that night. They filmed it.

"I would take a shower forever until the water went cold trying to feel clean, but I never felt clean. I still don't feel clean," she told me, looking down at the table.

"What is the biggest lie you have been told?" I asked.

"He loves me."

"Do you believe in love?" I asked.

"I used to. I lost my child…hold please…(shot of vodka)…I got pregnant. I got engaged to a man who came back from Iraq. His wife and child were killed in a car wreck. He would get all the way angry. One time, he got mad and slammed me against a bookshelf. He started punching me in the abdomen. I lost the baby. We were going to name him Michael Anthony." She eyed the vodka bottle.

I believe this was fiancée Number One. Fiancée Number Two was a pill popper and *all the way* meant times ten. He came home one day for lunch and couldn't find his phone. He blamed her and hit her in the ear. It busted her eardrum, and now she is deaf in the right ear. The police were called. For the third time.

"Never date anyone you meet in rehab!" she laughed. I looked at the guy in the corner. He sat motionless, staring at us. His hair was oily and flat on his head. Some teeth were missing. He looked rough.

"Who is your hero?" I asked, looking back at Elizabeth.

"My grandmother, but do you want to know why? Fuck…(cry)…y'all are getting me here. She is the only human that never had to raise her voice to get respect. So poised. So kind." Elizabeth's head slumped into her hands. She didn't want to cry.

Every time she mentioned her grandmother, she would start to cry. Start, but not actually cry. She would bury her face into her hands, take a deep breath, and mumble *"toughen up, soldier"* before regaining her composure.

After the gang rape, she took the morning after pill. Her strict Catholic family disapproved and would not allow her to attend her grandmother's funeral.

"Do you like pancakes?" I asked, trying to lighten up the conversation.

"No," she replied. Never mind. Back to the hard stuff.

"What hurts most in your body?" I tried not to scan her body with my eyes for imperfections.

"My colon. When I go number two it is unpleasant. Embarrassing. Frustrating. Obnoxious." Her voice softened.

At one point in our three-hour interview, she told me to turn off the recorder I was using to capture our conversation. She had to go to the bathroom and didn't want the recorder to pick up the noises. A beautiful twenty-eight-year-old girl… worried about the noises from a diseased colon.

When she returned from the bathroom, she talked about the most recent guy she dated who looked like The Rock and kept her captive in a van. He reversed the locks, installed cameras, and hid the van away from populated areas so nobody could hear her. He rolled his own cigarettes and cut them with meth. He gave her the meth-laced cigarettes and watched her have seizures all alone in the van. She lived in the van for six months. He eventually dropped her off at a hotel. Now he is in prison, and she was relocated to Nashville through the court system.

"How many times have you been in love?" I asked.

"Clearly many times with the wrong person. Does it include puppies and animals?" she said, trying to change the subject.

"Do you still believe in love?" I continued.

"Fifty-fifty. Do I think I will find it? No. There are far too many issues. PTSD, manic depression, seizures, cancer, and HIV. I try to make people not fall in love with me because I would only be a burden to them."

It took her almost an hour before admitting she was HIV positive. She said it softly and then said she had hand sanitizer if we wanted it, suggesting we might be scared of her. It was heartbreaking.

"What is your favorite flower?" I smiled.

"The sunflower. It grows so tall. It grows so strong. And no matter the weather, it still blooms," she replied without hesitation. Great answer, I thought. Mine too.

"Have you ever done heroin?" I didn't see tracks on her arm but knew drug use was common in homeless communities.

"No. I hate that stuff. My friend died in my arms with a needle stuck in her arms. The paramedics took thirty-three minutes and twenty-three seconds to arrive. They told me to shoot cold water into her vein with the needle. I didn't know how to do that! They told me to put her in a cold shower. The people at the party told me to put her body in the alley in the back. I couldn't save her! Her mother looked me in the eye and said, "She trusted you." It was after my grandmother died, and I was all the way fucked up. I can still see her face. I should have saved her." She shut her eyes and angrily wiped away new tears.

She took a shot of vodka (probably shot number ten).

"Can we take a break?" she asked me, seeming a little tired.

"Of course," I replied, looking around the room at the others. She walked outside to smoke a cigarette. The homeless man in the corner stared at us, motionless. Ty Ty, the homeless woman in the bed, snored like a train.

Once back in the room and settled at the table, I asked her a question I had been debating. "Are you afraid of dying?"

"To be honest, I was at first. I'm not gonna lie. I've been right with the Lord. Every time I lay my head on the pillow or the cement, I know I've done nothing but try to be the best I can be. So I'm no longer afraid. Every once in a while, I get scared with my health issues...to be alone. I try to be the best I can be and pay it forward. Overall, I'm not scared. It took many months to overcome it, but I've got this," she said in a hopeful voice.

"What scares you the most?" I continued.

"Bugs. I hate bugs. I can whoop anybody's ass, but I hate bugs. A boy put a cicada on my shoulder on the bus in elementary school, and I freaked out. I all the way hate bugs." Her big smiled returned. I laughed. I could see the little girl in her. She was beautiful.

We were about two hours in, and I could tell she was getting tired. How could she not? She held her side the whole time as we talked. I am not sure if it was from the cancer or her liver. She said her side hurt all the time.

"I wouldn't change any part of my life. It has been hard. I wouldn't want anyone else to have to go through it." A forced smile formed on her face.

At that point, Ilene put her head in her hands.

It was approaching three hours, and I told her I had one last question.

"What do you love the most about yourself?"

She couldn't answer. We all sat in silence.

Tears ran down her face, and she hid her face in her hands again. "I hate these questions. When you've been told you're a piece of shit all the time, it gets embedded in your brain. I'm all the way disappointed in myself. You want an honest answer? I don't know anymore. The only thing I love about myself is I still have the ability to care about other people. I don't want to see anybody hurt or suffer. I still have that quality even though I should be all the way bitter."

This was the only time I silently cried in the three hours we were together.

At the end, she asked why we dropped everything to come see her.

I stumbled over my words and told her I wanted to learn how to love.

In a soft and comforting voice, she asked, "Can I give you one bit of advice?"

"Of course." I wiped the tears from my face.

"Mind over matter. Even when you are all the way hurting, somebody always has it worse than you. That should be the mentality and the motivation for you to overcome it. You are all the way a goofball, and funny, and kind, and have a great smile, and great laugh. Don't dwell on the cards you have been dealt in your life."

Damn you, girl.

We took her to the store to buy some cigarettes and apple juice when we were done. She asked for the receipt so she could pay me back.

The road to self-love can be a difficult one. A beautiful girl beaten down by the world taught me love in a dirty hotel room full of despair and pain. Her body was losing the race, but her was heart was winning. If she can look inside herself and find love, then so can I. Sometimes it takes the story of another to help us heal ourselves.

The path to self-love starts with finding kindness for ourselves. The kindness we would show a new friend. This was the path I was on when I met Elizabeth. I don't think anyone can destroy a heart as big as Elizabeth's.

We all just want to be loved. All the way.

LOVE LESSONS

1. When we can't figure out how to love ourselves, we should start by finding compassion and empathy for others.

2. The road to self-love starts with simple kindness, empathy, and compassion for ourselves. The ability to not critically judge ourselves. The first step is trying to just be a friend to ourselves. A casual friend.

3. There is always someone who has it worse than you do. Find them and listen to their story. Ask people how they are doing. Then ask them again until they tell you the truth.

7

JOLLY MEETS
MOTORMOUTH

———

*"If you eat the green bananas they don't taste as good, so be
patient with bananas and with love."*

– ISABELLA, THIRTEEN YEARS OLD

I could smell him. He smelled like muddy socks and dirty
van carpet. His smile was pulling down his ears. Happiness
radiated from his eyes. This dude has it, the thing we all
want. Unbridled joy.

We sat beside his small school bus. His blonde, curly hair
was pulled back in a small ponytail. He had a broad chest
beneath an old button-up shirt.

I traveled two hours outside of Atlanta to meet him. He
might just be the happiest person in the world. Clearly, he
would have an interesting take on love, I thought. His bus
was parked behind an abandoned building. What was once
a small school bus was now a traveling hippie house for two.
His wife rolled out of the dark, abandoned building with a

glass of homemade kefir. She was beautiful with long, dark hair and a smile to match. I had no idea what kefir was but decided to taste it. It was chunky.

"Kefir has a ton of healthy probiotics that are great for healing your gut," she proudly informed me. I didn't know my gut needed healing. I also wasn't sure how a ton of anything could fit in a small glass of rank milk.

Michael has always fascinated me. I had heard about him for years. He worked at a bar I bought before I owned it. To me, he was a mysterious legend who had lived adventures I envied. Oh, and he was always smiling. Always. His nickname is Jolly.

I am drawn to people who live unorthodox lives. People who live just outside of the box. I think that is where the magic is, just outside of the box.

"Have you ever not smiled?" I joked as we got seated in the worn-out lawn chairs beside his little bus.

"Haaaa!" He let out a big, belly laugh.

"Actually, I recently went through all my Facebook pictures. I counted 220 total pictures, and there were only two pictures where I wasn't smiling!" His head tilted back as he belted out another deep laugh. The dude always laughs.

"Now I don't use any social media. I dedicate all of my NOW time to "this" 3D world so I can be fully present for all those in front of me," he boasted.

A vintage table sat between us with a tea set. The sun was shining right in my eyes. I could feel them cooking. Birds off in the distance were singing their songs.

Michael, who goes by Jolly, has done some interesting things. He was adopted twenty-four hours after birth and spent the majority of his childhood trying to fit in. Dancing with the devil, his younger self dabbled in the usual—booze, drugs, and girls. Around the age of twenty-three, he hit a wall driving sixty miles per hour. Remarkably, the car crumbled around him and didn't leave a scratch.

"I called the police on myself." His eyes got big as he leaned toward me.

It was a turning point for him. He wanted more from life. After working in bars and clubs as a bouncer, he set off to hike the Appalachian Trail, a grueling 2190-mile trail on the East coast of the United States. It can take anywhere from four to seven months to hike the entire trail.[3] It is a demanding hike full of animals, mountains, rain, snow, and smelly hikers. Less than 20 percent finish the entire trail. He did. He was unsatisfied with the lackluster finish line, so he kept walking into Canada, traveling another seven hundred miles by foot. He might be the only human on earth to smile the entire time.

Next, he decided to scrape together five thousand dollars and ride a bicycle through all forty-eight continental US states. He practiced his people skills by playing poker four nights a week in the bar he managed. During his adventure he traveled couch to couch, meeting stranger after stranger.

"What was the hardest part of the trip?" I asked as I wiped some sweat from my forehead.

"When you start an adventure is when you are most likely to quit. I was crying as I crossed the seven-mile bridge in Key West on the first day," he laughed. Of course, he laughed. "Then a man actually caught me with his fishing rod and pulled me off my bike as I was crossing another bridge." He motioned getting yanked backward.

---

3   "The Adventure of a Lifetime: Thru-Hiking," Appalachian Trail Conservancy, accessed July 15, 2020.

Trying to understand how he persevered, I asked, "What kept you going?"

"In the panhandle of Florida, I stopped at a gas station. I was really down and wanted to quit. As I was leaving the gas station, a homeless guy named Motormouth ran up to me. I quickly read the book by its cover and realized he was on meth or some other drug. I immediately told him I didn't have any money."

His hands raised as he continued to act out the story. "No, what are you doing?" the homeless guy barked at Jolly.

"Well, three years ago I hiked the Appalachian Trail," Jolly said, slowly backing away.

"Oh man! I am an alcoholic and drug addict. I always tried to walk the Appalachian Trail, but I quit every time," the homeless guy shouted. "What are you doing now?"

"I am trying to ride this bicycle through all forty-eight states," Jolly replied, still on guard.

Jolly felt the homeless guy's energy shift.

In a flash, the homeless guy grabbed Jolly's shirt in a fist and pulled him in aggressively, eye to eye.

"I am a trier, and I failed," he yelled. "You are a doer! Don't ever say the word 'try' again! You do things and finish them."

I shifted in my lawn chair. I wasn't expecting that turn of events.

Jolly continued, "I never once doubted the fact that I was going to bicycle all forty-eight states from that moment. I had seven or eight days before that moment that were pretty rough, but because of that man, I became a finisher. He was the pebble that turned my wave around. Whatever you buy into, there's got to be a start and there's got to be a finish, and that day, he turned me into a finisher."

Jolly went on to explain how he never contemplated quitting again and finished all forty-eight states in nine months, racking up eleven thousand miles. He only stayed in a hotel five nights. The rest were spent in tents on the side of the road and strangers' couches.

Since he has traveled the world, married a beautiful woman from the Netherlands, and lived life on his terms. Smiling the whole time, of course. He never stays in the same place long and is not interested in corporate jobs. His passion is bringing joy to the world. That is a big order, but he is a big order filler.

Isn't it amazing how powerful a few encouraging words can be? Kindness from a homeless guy outside a gas station propelled a man eleven thousand miles and beyond.

A pebble turned a wave around.

We finished up our chat after a couple of hours. My face was on fire from sunburn. I checked out the inside of his little bus. It was like a hippie sanctuary. Bed, sink, boho-style décor, and little handmade pieces of art saying 'love' and 'kindness' and other hippie things.

"We are "modern-day hippies," taking the successes of the old but evolving it into our own song for the NOW," Jolly said about him and his wife. Very hippie-ish.

As I was leaving, he slipped a small bag into my hand. "That is the good stuff, man. Made by love with love! It is 'Rainbow Fluff', either you KNOW or you will say no. Have fun!" he said with a monster smile.

"What is it?" I asked, staring at the small, clear bag containing a small piece of paper.

"The purest LSD in the world!" He grabbed me and pulled me in for a big hug. That's the thing about Jolly, he loves big. From the moment I arrived to the very last hug, he radiated love and joy.

I have always thought hippies love better than non-hippies. They are always smiling. Maybe it is the drugs. Maybe it is because they don't compare their lives to others. Maybe it is because they go on wild adventures around the world and connect with people like a homeless man at a convenience store. Maybe it is because they truly understand how to cultivate love, joy, and happiness.

My conversation with Jolly was a great reminder of how powerful a tiny act of kindness can be for someone else. A small pebble of appreciation or encouragement can travel the entire world. It was also a reminder to live our lives how we wish to, not how others wish we would.

As I was leaving, he said, "When you can find inner PEACE then you will realize that you have always been a MASTER piece to this beautiful puzzle called LIFE. I love you, man."

I love you too!

LOVE LESSONS

1. When we compare our lives to others, we never win. Live the life you would love to live. Your happiness comes from doing what you love on your own terms. Comparison robs us of joy. If I base my happiness by comparing my life to someone else's, I lose. If I wallow in the fact I am not in love, I have difficulty with love, and get upset because I assume it is easy for everyone else because of their Instagram pictures, I will go insane. When I start loving my life, it attracts love into my life. Like attracts like.

2. Give out pebbles every day. In the coffee shop, in your home, or in your business. Everyone needs a little encouragement. Change the world one pebble at a time. Pour affirmations into others around you. Build them up. Give them strength. Make them finishers.

3. Say yes to adventures and connect with new people. Go to lunch with someone new every day for thirty days. Travel solo for two weeks. Join a new club. Get comfortable being around new people. People teach us how to love and then let us practice on them.

8

THE REBEL RABBI

———

"Love is like bananas because when you open it up, it feeds you...like love."

SOPHIE, FOURTEEN YEARS OLD

The community center was enormous. I had to pass through a checkpoint gate to enter. Tennis courts and other recreational areas were spread across the large campus. I parked my car and entered the main building that housed racquetball courts, offices, and a small cafeteria.

I had arranged to meet the rabbi at the community center. My friend Ilene told me about him. She said he was an ex-sex therapist turned rabbi turned director of one of the largest Jewish community centers in New York. He sounded like an interesting dude. Someone who had love figured out, I guess.

He appeared in the hallway and greeted me. He didn't look like a rabbi. He did not have a long, white beard and was not wearing robes. He wasn't old. He looked like a normal dude and not a character from *Game of Thrones*.

We went into a large, empty cafeteria and sat at a plastic folding table. His hair never moved. It was thick and brown. Perhaps a toupee. Perhaps not.

"I am excited," he announced enthusiastically.

"Me too. Thanks for meeting with me." I tried to match his excitement and energy.

We settled into the conversation, and he told me why he became a rabbi. When he was in his early twenties, he found a mentor who was a Russian rabbi. The mentor asked him what he wanted to do with his life. He told the rabbi he loved selling.

"I thought, I could sell key chains or Judaism. And it was Palm Beach, Florida. So, the allure of a normal salary was also exciting. This rabbi was wearing all these gold chains and a gold watch, and I thought wow, cool. I want a Mercedes. Maybe this is the way. Because prior to that, my image of a rabbi was always a poverty-stricken, pious individual who would be crouched over studying the Bible all the time. I told him that I love sales, and he told me to become a rabbi because the hardest challenge in the world was selling Judaism." His voice remained animated. The dude was bursting with energy.

We laughed together as he made fun of himself and the fact he had no filter. He had me laughing the entire time.

"What is the key to happiness?" I asked, looking around the massive cafeteria room.

"Happiness is so overrated. You know, maybe it's the search for happiness or the search for self- fulfillment. I think it's self-fulfillment, and self-actualization, and healthy rela-tionships. I think those create an atmosphere of happiness. You know, because sometimes the rejoicing itself will lead to a sense of happiness or fulfillment. I just think happiness is overrated, and why bother looking for it? It's the search for fulfillment that leads to happiness. I'd rather use the term 'rejoice' than happiness. Rejoicing leads to happiness." His answers bounced around as he pieced his thoughts together. He was quirky and jittery, like an antsy teenager in an amusement park.

"Have you ever tried LSD?" I asked to test his weirdness. Do religious figures do drugs? I have no idea. Probably.

"No," he replied.

Guess not.

"It was because I'm such a dork. I was never around that stuff. I grew up in a Jewish school and went to a Jewish high school. It just wasn't happening in my community. I do regret that I did not have certain opportunities in my life. A part of me wishes I had dabbled a little bit just to know what that world was like." He touched his chin in wonder.

We continued to talk for the next hour. He was all over the place. His voice was powerful and playful like a kid, saying whatever came to mind. At one point he blurted out he didn't want to be talking to me. He said he had a kidney stone and was in massive pain. Then his head fell back in laughter. A quirky man. I liked him.

"Do you believe in soulmates?" I asked.

"No, no. I don't. No." He spoke as he thought about it. "I mean, it's a Jewish concept. You know, the idea that we were created when God created the heavens, then Earth, and that humanity was formed as one androgynous unit and split in half. The thought is that we spend our lives or a portion of our lives finding that other half. That's a soulmate. But I do not believe in that. I believe we find another person with whom we are compatible and with whom we can forge a relationship and spend a life with. So, no." He paused and looked at me. "Did that answer surprise you a little bit?"

"Well, no, not really. I have no idea if soulmates exist, but I like your answer." My brain was trying to keep up with the conversation.

I eventually asked him about love. I assumed if anyone knew about love it would have to be an ex-sex therapist turned rabbi who married a doctor of psychology.

"What is the definition of love?" I asked.

"I knew you were going to ask me that," he laughed. "I decided not to research it. I have no clue. Here's what I know, though. It has no definition. It is like, what is God? We don't know. Here's how I will explain it. If we go outside and see the trees and leaves blowing, we can't see the wind but know it's there. It's invisible. I feel like love is the same way. We know it's there. We can't define it. We can't necessarily even identify it, but we feel it in a profound, beautiful, magical way."

Wow, I thought. It is undefinable, yet we do feel it. It is like God. Beyond us.

"What advice do you give single people?" I looked down at the notes I couldn't read because my handwriting is horrific.

"Like dating? I was single for a period of time, and I remember that I was just feeling so desperate and lonely, and I felt like I needed somebody. That's when I was making the worst decisions and finding the wrong people. And then I said, 'Forget all of that,' and I focused on me and doing good things like volunteering and getting involved in charities and religiosity. And then, lo and behold, you know, that's when I started meeting the people that I needed to meet," he said. He joked by following his comment with, "Duh!"

I was running out of time, and he was in serious pain even though he seemed to be having fun with the interview. An assistant popped her head in the door and told him his next meeting was in fifteen minutes.

"How do people have better sex?" I bravely asked, knowing he was a sex therapist early in his twenties. It felt odd asking a rabbi about sex.

"With toys, equipment, lube, different ports of entry" he fired back quickly with a laugh.

When we were finally done, we both got up from the table, and as I was packing my bag with my gear, he leaned over and said, "You didn't ask me if I believe in God."

"You are right," I said, "Do you believe in God?"

"No. I don't believe in a fatherly image in the sky or a man in robes sitting in the clouds. I believe that what we call God is upon us, inside us, and around us. It is here and now. It is love."

LOVE LESSONS

1. Happiness is overrated. Self-fulfillment, self-actualization, and healthy relationships lead to happiness. If we focus on rejoicing, happiness is the by-product. Seek to be a joyful person who practices gratitude and rejoicing. Create a rejoicing ritual. Write ten things you are grateful for every morning.

2. We have to be in a healthy place before we can find the right person for us. We must get involved in helping others and finding our passions. When we are healthy, we attract healthy people into our lives. Volunteer, join groups, and seek what lights you up.

3. The key to better sex is sex toys.

9

A HUNDRED YEARS

———

"Love everyone because even rotten bananas are good in banana bread."

– EMILY, EIGHT YEARS OLD

I was nervous. He looked confused, sitting motionless in a small chair. His hands rested neatly in his lap as he sat straight up with his shoulders back. Perfect posture. The place smelled like processed food and grandparents. People meandered around the open foyer, a large lobby area of an apartment building. Ralph sat patiently, scanning the room with his eyes.

"Hi." I introduced myself as I walked up to him.

"Hello," he replied softly with a humble smile, looking up at me. His knit shirt was tucked perfectly into his khaki pants. A pair of glasses rested on his nose. His hair was neatly combed to the side.

"Maybe we should go to my room where it is quieter," he said to me in a hushed voice.

"Sounds good to me." I flashed my best smile.

I followed him to the elevator. It took a while for him to get there. The doors finally opened, and we crammed in with several other people. No one spoke except an old lady in the back corner who insisted on telling everyone to "have a wonderful day." She was wearing her pants backward and a hat as loud as a parade.

I took a seat at a small table in his apartment. The place was well-organized and spotlessly clean. Two bedrooms book-ended a small living room and kitchen. Paintings covered the walls and the couch looked like it had never been used. A small 1970s TV sat on a small 1970s TV stand.

Ralph was born in Canada in 1917. He met his wife of fifty years when he was a teenager. She waited for him during his four-year deployment in World War II. After the war, they moved to Atlanta, Georgia. In 1996, his wife died after suffering a stroke at a professional basketball game. He got in a car accident on the way to the hospital to see her. I had arranged an interview with him through the assisted living center where he has lived for the last twenty-five years, or since his wife died. Ralph was 101 years old when we sat down to talk. He looked sixty-five years old. His handshake was stronger than mine.

He sat patiently, not offering any small talk.

"I don't know why you want to talk to me," he said as we started. He had not been interviewed before. He seemed timid about the whole process.

"I am talking to people about love and life. I thought it would be fun to hear your perspective." I spoke softly, trying to match his energy.

"Okay," Ralph said with no emotion. Just a basic "okay." Okay, here we go.

"What is the key to happiness?" I asked right out of the gate. He seemed like a happy guy.

"Luck." Nothing further. No more words. He just said 'luck' and stared at me, waiting for the next question. I could tell he was not used to meeting random strangers, letting them in his apartment, and answering the most daunting questions of all time.

"If you could do anything in the world, with no limitations, what would it be?" I asked from across the tiny table.

"Walk. I used to love walking, but I had a heart attack in 2011. I now have six stents in my heart and get tired too easily. All I can do now are push-ups," he said defeatedly.

"Push-ups?" I looked up from my notes.

"Yeah. I do seventy-five push-ups every morning when I wake up," Ralph said nonchalantly, as if a one hundred-year-old man crushing seventy-five pushups every morning is COMPLETELY NORMAL.

I about fell out of my chair. Ralph was born in 1917, has a half-dozen stents in his heart, and does seventy-five pushups every morning. I have zero heart stents, am fifty-three years younger, and couldn't do twenty push-ups if you offered me a brick of pure gold.

I learned he loves peanut butter, makes his own breakfast and lunch, and reads four hours a day.

"I stopped driving when I turned one hundred, but my new driver's license is valid through 2025!" he said with a rare laugh.

His favorite place to visit was the Galapagos Islands. His favorite hobby is painting. He goes to sleep every night at 11:30 p.m. after watching the news and wakes up every morning around 8:00 a.m. He has a drink at night before dinner, preferring Seagram's VO, H&H, or vodka.

"What is the meaning of life?" I smiled.

"Oh…I'm not a philosopher. I have no idea. To live?" His eyebrows raised.

"Do you have a best friend?" I continued.

"No."

"You married your high school sweetheart and were married for fifty years. What is the key to a happy marriage?" I glanced over at a black and white framed picture of his wife and him on the wall.

"You have to think of the other person more than yourself. My marriage was 95 percent ups with only 5 percent downs." He looked off like he was revisiting his wife in his mind. "I loved her cooking, especially her meatloaf." He smiled.

"That's great." I hate meatloaf.

He continued to talk about his wife. "She was my one and only love. We would go on a dinner date once a week, every week, for fifty years."

Wow, I thought. I keep hearing this one-date-a-week rule from people I interview who are in healthy, long-term relationships. I have decided if I get in a long-term relationship, I want to implement this rule. I think some relationships fall apart because we don't dedicate, schedule, and spend quality time together on a regular basis.

"What is the definition of love?" I asked, winding down the interview.

"There's not one," he said confidently.

I loved his answer. How could there be? Love is too powerful to be defined. It is what it is. It is like defining God or the universe. It is bigger than humans can comprehend.

I had been with him for around an hour. I could tell he was getting either tired or annoyed with me. I leaned in for one final question. "What is the best gift to give someone?"

"Love," he whispered with a smile.

Ralph, a man of few words and a hundred years of experience, seemed to have it right. Life is pretty simple.

It reminded me to quit overthinking things. Don't complain. Make the best of what you've got. And above all, give love. I want to live like Ralph. Simple, loving, and doing seventy-five push-ups a day until the end. Oh, and maybe a cocktail here and there for good measure.

LOVE LESSONS

1. Start doing the things you love now before your body slows down and you can't do them anymore. We are all racing the clock. Don't let time win. Go do some fun shit.

2. Create a weekly ritual with the person you love. A dinner, lunch, walk, phone call, and so on. Pick the person closest to you (a wife, husband, best friend, sister, or other) and create a weekly ritual of connection.

3. Sit up straight, do seventy-five pushups a day, have a drink before bed, and you might just live forever.

10

ROCK AND FLOWER

"If you break the banana it is never the same with love so be careful not to break it."

— JACKSON, FOURTEEN YEARS OLD

"I'll go," I said reluctantly, trying to avoid eye contact with the others. My heart raced.

We were all sitting in a circle. It was a twenty-foot by thirty-foot room with thick, brown carpet and navy walls. The window shades were closed. My nerves were shot. It was day three of six. I was in a room full of strangers and terrified of what was coming next.

I was next.

Six of us filled the room. Well, seven including the woman in charge. She had dark eyes and the wisdom of Sigmund Freud. A triangle tattoo decorated both of her hands. She was wearing a mask because of the COVID-19 virus. I couldn't tell if she was smiling. I hoped she was smiling. We sat on big pillows. They wanted us to be comfortable while being uncomfortable.

In my efforts to figure out love, I decided to sign up for an expensive, week-long, therapeutic workshop at a swanky place in the Tennessee mountains. It has the reputation of being one of the best places in America to work on your shit. My shit needed working on. As usual.

The workshop was titled "Love & Relationships." The campus was a sprawling farm with several cabins and a large plantation house. The food was amazing; three meals a day of organic Southern vegetables and delicious meats. They even had a snack room loaded with goodies. It was not a place to lose weight.

There were horses. I never touched them. Horses have big teeth.

After lunch, the therapist told us to go into the woods and find something that represented how we felt coming into the week and something to represent how we wanted to feel leaving at the end of the week. The guy next to me asked if he could bring in horse shit.

Easy, I thought, as she dismissed us into the wild. I would grab a rock to represent me coming into the week—hard and closed off—and then find a flower to represent me leaving the week—open and soft. Boom! Perfect. Honor student. Homerun. No crying. God, I hate crying.

Most of my life I have been closed off, especially to love. I have guarded my heart by avoiding anything that has to do with feelings. Like this retreat. However, I desperately wanted to open my heart so I could find love and connection with others. Easier said than done.

I wandered off to the woods to look for my objects. It was blazing hot, so I wanted to grab them quickly and get back in the room with air conditioning. I found a nice, smooth, white rock as I poked around where the grass met the tree line. I chose white because white represents hope.

I continued along the edge of the woods and found a beautiful purple flower. It was the size of a large man's hand, with lots of small, rounded petals extending into the air. The center was a warm yellow. The petals were a lavender purple. The perfect flower, I thought. They are going to be so impressed back in the room.

With my two perfect objects in hand, I started back toward the meeting room. Then the damn thing appeared and wrecked my plan.

I looked down in the short grass next to where I was standing and saw a huge, black snake sitting motionless, staring right at me. I froze.

It was a beautiful snake. Black as night and as thick as a Coke bottle. Six or seven feet, at least. We locked eyes for what seemed like an eternity. It didn't move. I didn't move. Instantly I knew the importance of the snake. Damn it.

I tried to move the snake with a stick. It didn't budge. It just followed my every move with its head. Eyes glued on me. Most snakes in the wild want to get away from you as quickly as possible. This one didn't. Odd, I thought.

Taking a snake into the room was a bad idea, so I left it alone and headed back. I couldn't get it out of my mind. The damn black snake.

"Okay, if you would like, each of you can come up and tell us about your objects," the therapist instructed. "Place the object representing you coming into the week on this side of the room and the object representing you leaving the week on the other side of the room" She spoke while pointing to each side, building an imaginary timeline.

Then she put a large, rectangular block in between the objects. It was about four feet tall and two feet wide. "This represents what is blocking you from how you want to be when you leave this place," she said, leaning on the big block. "We need to figure out what it is."

Shit.

I contemplated not telling the group about the snake. I knew exactly why I saw it in the woods. If I brought it up, it was going to get ugly. I didn't want it to get ugly. I wanted to just show my rock and the flower, be done, and sit back down.

Fuck it.

I stood up with my rock and flower. I also took the black strap off my messenger bag. That would represent the snake.

I placed the rock on one side of the room and the flower on the other. Then I placed the black strap on top of the block.

I stood next to the block. The rest of the group sat at their seats. I started shaking. I took a deep breath.

"So, the rock represents me coming into the week. Hard and closed off," I started without making eye contact with anyone in the room. My voice was shaky. "The flower is how I want to be leaving next week, open and soft." Another deep breath.

I paused. The pause seemed like forever.

I won't go into the embarrassing details about my experience, but I decided to tell them about the snake. When I did, tears exploded from my eyes and I buried my head in my hands. I cried for several minutes. I stood there, in the center of the room, crying into my hands. All eyes on me. Broken, scared, and vulnerable. My worst hell on earth.

Eventually I pulled it together enough to open my eyes. The therapist told me to sit down in front of the block. She sat down in front of me and looked deeply into my eyes. We were inches apart.

"You are easy to love," she said in a soft, compassionate voice. Over and over. "You are easy to love." I stared into her eyes. Tears rolled down my face. I didn't care.

The thing is, at one point, I believed her.

The hard thing about hard things is they are fucking hard. In that room, in front of those people, exposing my heart was one of the most difficult things I have ever done. A lifetime of pain expressed in one moment of time.

When I was a little boy, my dad took me to a pet shop. He asked the owner to pull out a huge snake and put it on my shoulders. A moment I will never forget. I loved every second of it. I can still remember how the snake felt on my shoulders.

The snake I saw in the woods was my dad. He was there to tell me to keep fighting, to keep showing up and doing the hard work, and to go back into that room and open my heart. I did, and it broke me wide open. I put the snake on the block. And from the top, my dad watched me find love for myself in a therapist's eyes.

Not all adventures are the fun kind. Some are the hard kind.

Maybe I am easy to love.

LOVE LESSONS

1. I have learned the hardest part of love is simply showing up. Showing up for myself and showing up for others. It requires me to show up for hard things. To do hard things. It requires going through pain to find healing.

2. I have learned to heal I must be vulnerable. I must push through fear and let people see my real heart. When I do, I realize I am not the only one who is scared. When I do, I feel loved.

3. I have learned everything we want in life is just on the other side of our fears. To see our biggest fear and walk right into the damn thing is the path to freedom and love. Everything we want is just on the other side of this invisible killer called fear.

11

SELF-THERAPY GUIDE

---

*"Bananas are like love because yellow is my favorite color
and bananas are yellow so I love them."*

– JULIA, FOUR YEARS OLD

I did drugs. Illegal drugs. Don't tell anyone.

A few years ago, I decided I wanted to try drugs for the first time. I have always been fascinated with drugs but never tried any because I was terrified I would jump off a building or microwave my head.

I was especially fascinated with the drug Ecstasy because it was referred to as the "love drug." I kept hearing people say it makes them happy, loving, and touchy-feely. Well, I could use some happy, loving, and touchy-feely in my life. So I decided one of my New Year's Eve resolutions was to try drugs.

A few months later I tried Ecstasy. To this day, it was the single greatest night of my entire life. I French kissed the girl of my dreams at an electronic DJ show on the dance floor of a Country and Western bar. Yup, a middle-aged man at a rave, in a country bar, kissing a girl on the dance floor. Don't judge me. Fine, judge me.

A few years later I tried it again in Las Vegas. However, this time all my friends went to sleep so I hid in the bathroom and interviewed myself. I wondered what I would say if I asked myself hard questions in a state of joy and ecstasy. So since I was bored and sleepless, I asked myself a bunch of questions. I recorded the answers in my phone.

My self-interview:

(Trey on drugs, 3:11 a.m., Las Vegas, in the bathroom of the MGM Grand Hotel.)

Trey: The question is...do you love yourself?

Trey: No, I don't.

Trey: Why?

Trey: Well. I feel like a failure in very important areas of my life...relationships...money...jobs...Mom....marriage...love.

Trey: Do you really think you have failed?

Trey: Yes.

Trey: Is there a god?

Trey: I think so.

Trey: Are you worth a shit?

Trey: I think so. Deep down I have a kind and caring heart. That's all I've got.

Trey: Why are you sad?

Trey: Because I compare myself to others. Because I'm not sure what to do with my life. All my other friends are having a great life, and I'm lost. I also feel lonely but I'm too shy to hit on girls and too fucked up for a real relationship.

Trey: What do you know?

Trey:

- I know there are people that care about me.

- I know there is a bizarre chemistry with my mom even though I love her the most.

- I know life is a lot harder than I thought it was going to be.

- I know I love dance music.

- I know I can make people feel good about themselves.

- I know in twelve years I will have outlived my dad's life.

- I know I'm scared a lot.

- I know the vision I have for myself is terrible and awesome.

Trey: What are you scared of?

Trey: Getting old is scary. I'm serious.

Trey: What are you thankful for?

Trey: So I'm thankful for my life. This year started on a beach in Thailand and then Vegas, South Africa, and Zambia. My bar is doing well, and my restaurant is starting to make money. Maybe this year will also include love. My mom hopes. I hope.

Trey: What else?

Trey: There is nothing else on earth that matters but love. Maybe that is all God is—love. The energy of love.

Trey: What do you want to do?

Trey: Man, I wish I could break my walls down.

Trey: Anything else?

Trey: I think my heart is right. It's just buried beneath layers of pain and protection. So I will continue to be good and kind to people. That's all I can do. The feeling right now on this drug is what I have always wanted and continue to want for my whole life. Pure love.

End.

As I look back on that conversation, I realize all I have ever wanted is love. I did not love myself but I have come a long way. I don't love myself all the time. For me it is a practice. I have to make an effort to love myself every day.

I think we can all learn to love ourselves with a little practice. Sometimes it takes experiences to start the process and experiences to continue the process.

Love is a practice, and it starts with ourselves.

YOUR TURN!

SELF-THERAPY 101

You know yourself better than anyone else. So I want you to schedule a time and be your own therapist. It is a lot cheaper. This radical experiment requires three things:

1. Mind-altering substance (Beer, spinach juice, coffee, essential oil, energy drink, or vodka martini).

2. Journal (Favorite journal and favorite pen).

3. Private area is quiet (Preferably not a Las Vegas bathroom).

Write a question. Then answer the question. Take your time, be honest, don't judge.

2

LOVE IS A
BATTLEFIELD

12

LOVE IS ADVENTURE

———

Let's do some crazy shit. Live loud. Break rules and love hard. Drink banana smoothies and add rum. My adventures have taken me all over the world. In this part of the book, we talk shoes and drink a cup of poison. Then I go into a snake's den, have an overdose, and break in a room full of strangers. Adventure is a doozy. Love is not a problem to be solved but an adventure to be had...

13

JUST DO IT

"I love bananas because they look like boomerangs."

– JARED, ELEVEN YEARS OLD

Gary was an idiot. Nancy was a stiff. Dan was a nerd. Somehow, someway, their lives collided and now we have the solu-
tion to love. Shoes.

Gary was a basket case. A bonified outlaw raised by an
abusive father and a suspect mother. Then, on the morning
of January 17, 1977, five bullets pierced his chest and lodged
into the sandbags behind him. The crazy bastard literally
asked for it. He was thirty-six years young.

In 1986, Nancy uttered a few words that would radicalize
America. Her husband was a movie star. He was shot once in
the chest by a deranged lunatic. He survived.

Dan is very smart and has never been shot. Lucky bastard.

Love is a battlefield. It is complicated, crazy, and confusing. It is uncontrollable and controllable. We have no power
over love but the power to love. It's a sweet, golden, goofy
mess. As I ventured into my journey of figuring out love, I
knew it was going to be hard. How could it not be? If it were

JUST DO IT · 87

easy, I would be a master already. Well guess what? I am not a master already.

Gary, Nancy, and Dan are three strangers with wildly different stories and one extremely powerful message. I believe this simple message is one of the keys to figuring out love.

Nancy wanted us to "just say no." Gary wanted the firing squad to "do it." Dan decided to combine both statements and came up with the greatest tagline in the history of business. "Just Do It."

When asked how he came up with a new tagline for Nike in 1988, Dan Wieden said he stole it from Gary Gilmore. Gary was prisoner in the Utah State Prison and executed by a firing squad in 1977. His last words were "Let's do it," referring to the firing squad about to execute him. Professor Natalia Mehlman Petrzela reflected on Dan's curiosity about Gary Gilmore's last words—"He remembered his 'Let's do it' as this ultimate act of intention," Petrzela says. "And he just thought it was such a powerful statement." She goes on to explain, "But then the rest of 'Just Do It' comes from a very different source, which was Nancy Reagan's 'Just Say No' campaign. Wieden mashed those two up and put them together and came up with 'Just Do It.'"[4]

So Nike's tagline, which resurrected the company in 1988 and has inspired every athlete of the past thirty years, came from a man who murdered two people and the First Lady of the United States. Talk about a juxtaposition. Talk about overpriced shoes.

To love, we have to "Just Do It." Not "it" as in sex. Well, actually...I digress.

---

4   Martin Kessler, "The Story Behind Nike's 'Just Do It' Slogan (wbur 2020)" WBUR (blog), November 23, 2018.

For me, it is saying "yes" to experiences I know will be hard, like accepting love from others, or showing compassion and empathy. It is going against the internal anxiety that goes ballistic when I am forced to talk about feelings. It is saying "yes" to life, new people, and new experiences. I must be social, even though I am an introvert who would much rather sit alone in a small raft in the middle of the ocean reading self-help books rather than go to a dinner party with other humans.

The queen of vulnerability, Brené Brown, says, "To love someone fiercely, to believe in something with your whole heart, to celebrate a fleeting moment in time, to fully engage in a life that doesn't come with guarantees—these are risks that involve vulnerability and often pain. But, I'm learning that recognizing and leaning into the discomfort of vulnerability teaches us how to live with joy, gratitude and grace."[5] That is a fancy way of saying the only way to love is through vulnerability.

There are no guarantees. There will be pain, failure, disappointment, and heartbreak. There will be rejection, which is my number one fear in life. So I avoid it. Problem solved. And guess what, I have been single for the better half of eternity.

I have learned the only way I change is when I lean into discomfort and do hard things. It is when I say yes to adventure, especially the things that scare me, make me uncomfortable, or challenge me. Like writing this fucking book.

It is being okay with being vulnerable.

What do you need to experience in your life to create a shift? Therapy? Travel? Magic mushrooms? Yoga? Speed dating? Cooking class? Reading this book twice? Telling

---

5   Brené Brown, The Gifts of Imperfection: Let Go of Who You Think
     You're Supposed to Be and Embrace Who You Are. (Center City:
     Hazelden, 2010), Page 22, 23.

your family to go away? Forgiving your best friend? Leaving a twenty-year relationship to finally be happy again?

Just do it.

LOVE LESSONS

1. When fear shows up, it is simply a red flag trying to keep us safe. However, love is not safe. We can be rejected, hurt, exposed, and experience a wad of other gross feelings. However, good feelings come from love too. Love risks everything. Every moment of our lives we either choose love or fear. Choose love. Just do it.

2. When we say yes to adventure, we discover our passions and create connections with others. When we say no to adventure we sit in the basement playing warlord video games eating cheese puffs. If you are looking for your passion, purpose, or partner find some adventure…it is there.

3. Buy a pair of red shoes. Make them your power shoes. Wear them when you need extra confidence. Gift a pair of red shoes to someone you love.

14

HELL ON EARTH

———

"Love is just like bananas because they don't grow when it's too hot or too cold."

— LILY, SIXTEEN YEARS OLD

His eyes looked tired. He was staring at his phone. Waiting...

It was my third day in Yemen. He was my guide. A tour guide in the worst country on earth. A place where men live off rice and corruption and women hide behind black veils. A lawless country without a government. Or tourism.

We were sitting in a hot, empty room on the third floor of a cement building somewhere in the middle of Yemen. It had no power. He leaned against one wall and I leaned against the other. It was so hot my sweat was sweating.

My buddy Garrett had convinced me to travel to Yemen with him. He was on a mission to go to every country in the world. To do so, well, you have to go to every country in the world. Even the terrifying ones. I was on a mission to find the answers to love and not get kidnapped.

Aman, our guide, and not his real name due to security concerns, met us at the border a few days before. A driver picked us up at our hotel in Oman at three o'clock in the morning and quietly drove us two hours to a small border crossing. Aman slipped the border officials some cash and loaded us into a Toyota truck.

The first thing I noticed about him was his smile. It could light up a room. It hid his teeth which were as worn-out as the war. His gums were dark and black. His hair was sporadic and thin. Mostly missing. He dressed proudly in an old sports jacket and some khaki pants.

Aman leaned over and whispered to me when I met him at the border. "From now on, you will say you are Turkish. Your new names will be Sami and Yusef," he said, pointing to me and Garrett. "Also, try not to speak in public. We don't need to draw any attention to ourselves," he warned.

Welcome to Yemen.

"What's wrong?" I asked as we sat in the hot room.

He had been sitting on the hard floor and leaning against the wall since we arrived earlier in the afternoon. Garrett and I were not allowed to leave the building. His tank top undershirt hadn't come off in days and he constantly smoked cigarettes. He chewed khat, a leafy stimulant that was popular in places like Yemen, Saudi Arabia, and Somalia, instead of eating dinner.

"I am trying to keep you safe," he mumbled as the light from his phone screen illuminated his face in the dark. His right cheek was the size of a softball full of Khat.

At the time, Yemen was a lawless nation run by rebels, soldiers, bandits, and smugglers. It had no acting government, and the United States travel advisory simply said, "do not travel." There was no US Embassy and no way out if things went sideways. Fighting consumed the North and terrorists filled the South. Bedouins, bandits, and smugglers filled in the rest. We were hiding somewhere in the middle on our four-day tour into the heart of Yemen.

"There is a ten-thousand-dollar bounty for a tip off on Americans." His eyes met mine. They looked tired and worried.

"What?" I inched a little closer to him to make sure I heard correctly.

"Terrorists kidnap North Americans and ransom them for ten to twenty million dollars. They will pay locals five to ten thousand dollars for tips on the whereabouts of any Westerners in Yemen. That is a lot of money for people in Yemen." His eyes shifted back to his phone screen.

Wonderful, I thought. Then I wondered if he was going to sell us to terrorists.

"America doesn't negotiate with terrorists, and my mom doesn't have twenty million dollars, so who pays?" I asked uncomfortably.

"United Arab Emirates or Oman will pay the ransom on behalf of the United States, so they look good in the world's eyes." His eyes never left the phone.

That's nice of them. I felt a little better.

"Or ISIS will get you and make a video. You don't want that." His expression grew stern.

I felt a little worse.

He didn't sleep a wink during our first two nights together. Instead, he laid on the ground, checking his phone every thirty minutes with updates from his contacts around the country. They would tell him if there were any uprisings or rumors of bad guys in the area. He changed our route frequently, and we never stayed in the same place twice, or for a long period of time. He brought us food, answered every question we asked, dealt with curious men with guns, and smiled the entire time.

The next day, we were traveling along an endless two-lane highway through the barren, boring, lifeless, brown desert. I decided to ask him about love. I figured he might have some interesting insights, so I leaned across Garrett and asked, "Are you married?"

"Yes, and I have two children." His head popped up from a hot, bouncy nap. I was sitting behind the driver. Garrett was next to me riding bitch. Aman was next to Garrett, sitting behind the passenger seat. Three dudes sweating through the Yemen desert. He was still wearing his sports jacket.

"Do you love your wife?" Sometimes I ask the dumbest questions.

"Yes, I love her. I love my family very much. I am trying to raise enough money to get them out of Yemen. It is too dangerous here. I am scared every day," he whispered. His eyes told the whole story.

As I looked at him, a smile crept onto his face. "Do you want to hear a love story?" He rubbed his eyes and looked at me.

Hell yes, I do. "Sure!"

"When I was younger, I met woman from Canada. I was eighteen years old. She was the most beautiful girl I had ever seen. We fell madly in love. I planned on leaving Yemen and starting my life with her in Canada." His face was alive, vibrant, and smiling. His voice was bold and proud.

"It was a kind of love that makes your heart shake," he said as he put his hand on his heart and closed his eyes.

Damn. A love that makes your heart shake. A perfect way to describe falling in love.

"What happened?" I asked.

"My father found out I was planning on leaving Yemen with her to start my new life. So he burned my passport." His eyes caught mine. His smile disappeared.

We sat silently for a moment.

"My current marriage was arranged by my father. He chose the girl. I never saw the Canadian girl again and have never left Yemen." His head lowered, and he stared at his hands.

Here was a guy risking his life to try to safely show us the country he once loved. A man who lost the love of his life when his father burned his passport. A man desperately trying to make a little money to pay a five-thousand-dollar bribe and get his family out of the country.

"Yemen is Hell," he muttered as he turned his head to look out the window at the lifeless desert passing by. I felt terrible. I even felt guilty. Guilty I was born in America and he was born in Yemen. Guilty I got to leave that hellhole a few days later and he couldn't. Guilty I have plenty of hope, and he seemed to have very little.

The rest of the trip was an adventure. He kept us safe even though there were a few suspect situations involving guns, threats, and larking strangers. In the end, I have been unable to stop thinking about his words, *A love that makes your heart shake.*

What struck me about my new friend from Yemen was his kindness. This dude was living in hell, where there was no work to be had, but treated us with kindness every moment. We were his first tour in three years.

I will always admire his strength. Life had been a difficult journey for Aman filled with loss and hardship, and yet he continued to love his family and show kindness and love to a couple of strangers from America.

I want to be a man like him.

LOVE LESSONS

1. One key element of love is trust. I had to trust a guide who I had never met before to safely get us through Yemen and not sell us to the crazy bastards who make assassination videos. I trusted him and we developed a beautiful friendship.

2. Having a family he loved kept Aman fighting for a better life. What keeps you fighting for a better life? Who are you living for besides yourself? Your family? A friend?

3. One trick to connecting with strangers is to ask them if they are in love. I always ask this to taxi drivers, guides, and other people I meet during my travels. Are you in love? Everyone has a story, and each one will teach us a lesson. Aman had one of the most beautiful and painful love stories I had ever heard.

15

THE MONK'S HANDS

———

"Bananas are like love because if you put them in a smoothie, they hold everything together."

– NATHAN, SIXTEEN YEARS OLD

"Don't touch the Monk's hands," Jack said as I exited the car. He was wearing a dark blue suit, an older one. Maybe the only one he owned. Jack is a string bean. Huge smile, skinny as a rail, with the heart of an elephant.

"Come." He smiled and turned toward the temple.

It was late April. I was sweating through my shirt. Truthfully, I felt underdressed. I was wearing the only black t-shirt and long pants I had. There was no telling where I was. We headed toward a large, concrete temple next to an open-air pavilion swarming with people who were cooking food. It was a thousand degrees outside.

I followed Jack into the temple. We were late, so he didn't have time to explain. It was eerily quiet inside and full of people. Long rows of benches led up to the front of the room. A few dozen men in maroon robes sat cross-legged on a raised platform that stretched down the right side. They looked important.

There wasn't a hint of air conditioning in the joint. I followed Jack down the center aisle toward the front where there was a huge display of flowers surrounding a painting of a woman. The woman in the painting was his mother. I was at her funeral in a rural area of Thailand.

I met Jack a few years before. I started a travel company and hired him to help me. He was a seasoned travel guide, so I hired him to be my right-hand man for a ten-day tour. It was a smart move. He was the kind of guy you fall in love with immediately. Always smiling, always kind, and always making sure nobody died.

"Don't touch his hands," Jack whispered in my ear as he lined me up directly in front of the first monk. My eyes met the monk's eyes, and I took a breath. He looked serious and unamused. I was fresh out of the car and now standing before a monk, trying to remember the monk gift-giving rules. Sweat beaded up on my forehead. I handed the monk an offering, some food and a drink, without touching his hands, which I assume would have sent me straight to hell. Success, I thought.

Jack nodded and smiled as I turned back to him for the next set of instructions. He motioned for me to move to the next monk. No words, just a nod of the head. I did. Bow, hand the offering, bow again, move. Repeat. Don't touch the monks. Don't go to hell.

Two years prior to the funeral, I escorted a group of ten Adderall-fueled Americans all over Thailand. Jack was my saving grace. He helped me navigate the complexities of traveling around Thailand with a bunch of lunatics. I think the people on my tour slept a total of fourteen minutes in ten days. It was brutal. I had to keep them alive and out of Thai prisons. One day I took them to a drag show around two o'clock in the afternoon. I snuck off to the bathroom during the show, set my phone alarm for ten minutes, and took a nap on the toilet. Tour guide 101.

Jack was a rock star. He catered to everyone in the group like they were his own family. He never complained and always wore a smile as I would panic about missing trains, horrific hotels, or losing members. One girl got a rash from a monkey. She had boils on her arm, and I was trying to figure out how I was going to tell her mother she died of a monkey disease. Jack whipped up a little ointment and she was good to go.

Jack was overwhelmingly kind. One guy fell off his scooter and ripped up his shoulder and back. Jack gently treated his back every day for a week to help it heal. That was Jack, the kindest man in Thailand.

I took two groups to Thailand over the years. I always made sure Jack was by my side. As we were settling at the end of the second tour, Jack told me he had to head back to his hometown to prepare for his mother's funeral.

"Oh, I am sorry to hear about your mother," I quickly replied, wondering why he didn't mention it during our trip.

"Thank you," Jack said with his soft voice.

I paused, then asked, "When did she pass away?" I hoped it wasn't during our tour.

"Two years ago," he replied.

"What?" I tried to contain my confusion.

"In my tradition, we do not have funerals immediately," he said in slightly broken English.

"Oh, okay. Where do you keep the body?" I wondered if that was crossing the line. I also wondered where the hell you keep a dead body for two years.

"We kept the body at home." He looked up at me like that was common sense. Jack explained, as part of his Buddhist tradition, the family does not typically have the funeral when the person dies. They generally wait a year or two. That is unless the person died in a tragic way, which would drive them to cremate quickly to offset bad spirits.

Interesting, I thought. Horrifying as well.

As I imagined keeping a dead body in my house for two years, Jack asked, "Would you like to come to her funeral?"

"Sure."

I was honored. It solidified a deeper friendship that felt like a brotherhood to me. I am an only child and my connection to Jack felt like having a brother. I felt important and honored to be there for Jack.

After I made my way down the line of monks, I exited the temple. Outside, under the pavilion, friends and family cooked massive amounts of curry and other dishes for the guests. Massive stainless steel pots full of soups and other dishes filled the pavilion. Pot after pot of white rice had been placed on all of the tables. Women churned the big pots with massive, wooden spoons. Everyone sweated under the heat of the day.

I sat down at a table toward the back, and the food immediately started coming. Person after person brought me a plate of food. They would smile. I would smile back. At one point I counted eleven plates in front of me. I had no clue what any of it was. I just kept eating.

As the sun started to set, we moved back inside of the temple. I was so impressed with how Jack carried himself. He had been the coordinator all day long, greeting people, moving people around, and making sure the procession continued. I felt bad because I never saw him get a chance to grieve for his mother.

In the end, everyone lined up and we silently walked along the side to the front where the flowers and image of his mother stood. As we headed toward the front, we passed a basket of small, wooden flowers. I noticed each person grab one, so I did the same.

The line curved around the back of the flower display and up a slight incline. I realized I was about to pass the furnace where Jack's mother's body laid. It was a small opening in a large, concrete wall. Her box was in the middle.

"Say a prayer," Jack whispered to me as I stood before his mother.

I bowed my head and closed my eyes…

I pray for a peaceful journey for you. Your son is one of the most amazing men I have ever met in my life. He has taught me about love and grace in ways I have never experienced. I hope you are as proud of him as I am. Thank you for bringing him into the world. Amen.

I tossed my flower into the furnace and moved outside with the rest of the group. Jack went last and lit the fire.

I watched Jack closely as everyone stood outside of the temple. My heart was full because of my love and appreciation for his kind soul. My heart also broke a little realizing he was saying goodbye to his mother. He stood there, finally alone, looking up as the smoke drifted into the sky.

LOVE LESSONS

1. Kindness, above all, is a foundation of love. Jack's kindness reached me on a deep level. Create good karma by being a kind person. The fourteenth Dalai Lama famously said, "My religion is very simple. My religion is kindness."[6] Make it a goal to be the kindest person in every room you enter.

---

6 "Top 20 Most Inspiring Dalai Lama Quotes," Goalcast, accessed September 12, 2020.

2. It is an honor when we can show up for another during times of loss. It is not our job to make everything all right or heal the pain. It is not our job to know the right thing to say or not say. It is our job to simply stand beside those we love and support them during hard times. Just show up.

3. Always attend Buddhist funerals hungry.

16

CRYING AT COACHELLA

———

"Bananas grow in bunches because people love to be with other people."

– ETHAN, TEN YEARS OLD

Saying yes to adventure can take a left turn sometimes. There are always lessons to be learned in love and life, some are completely bananas. Like the time I encountered something so deadly, so lethal, it damn near killed me.

Perhaps you have heard of the number one killer of all human beings, animals, aliens, and plants…marijuana. If not, let me explain. Marijuana is a plant, grown in HELL, and full of ingredients that MAKE YOU WANT TO DIE. It's consumed by roughly 125 percent of all teenagers around the world. Now that you are an expert, let's talk about my overdose at the Coachella Music Festival, the single worst day of my life.

Let me begin by stating I don't usually do drugs. I'm not against drugs, but too much of a pansy to do them because I watched to many "this is your brain on drugs" commercials with fried eggs when I was younger. However, I did smoke Marlboro cigarettes in a Mexican prison one time.

Side Note: I didn't try alcohol until I was twenty-four years old. Therefore, I didn't meet any girls until I was twenty-four years old. You know that loser friend you had in college who didn't drink? Yep. Me.

Onward…

The first time I experienced this deadly narcotic was in a small and colorful beach town in Southern Costa Rica called, well, I can't remember. However, I do remember a bunch of gay cowboys riding around on horses draped in rainbow colors as our beat-up city bus pulled into town. The town was alive with music and festivities. We had traveled along a tedious road through the mountains from the capital city of San Jose for hours.

I was traveling with two girlfriends. Both gals were extremely attractive and extremely unattracted to me. My chances of hooking up with either one of them hovered around 0 percent. The tiny beach town had a Bob Marley vibe and plenty of weed so the girls loaded up upon arrival. Later that night, they held me down and blew smoke in my face until I got a contact high. Literally.

I remember feeling strange as the narcotic took effect. My body started tingling and my brain slowed down. I Laughed. A lot.

So this is what being stoned feels like, I thought. Not bad.

Fast-forward six months to Southern California where I found myself at Coachella, a music festival in California that hosts a billion bands and a trillion people who looked like they robbed an Urban Outfitters store. Oh, and Brad Pitt. Keep reading…

I was staying at a roadside hotel with four girls. Two twenty-one-year-old hippies, a hippie clothing designer, and my friend Jakie, whose name I purposely misspelled to protect her identity. All four girls were super attractive and GUESS WHAT? They were all unattracted to me. Shocker.

On Saturday, we were getting ready to leave the hotel and head to the music festival. The hippie chicks (who had bought all the marijuana in the entire state of California) whipped out a medicinal marijuana brownie the size of a sandwich. It had a warning label. I don't read warning labels. I bet you thirty-four dollars and a used Corvette you can't guess what happened next.

I ATE THE WHOLE FUCKING THING.

Let me remind you this was the second time in my pathetic life I had ever tried marijuana. Also let me inform you this was the first time I ever tried "edible" marijuana.

I remember feeling relaxed once the toxins started invading my bloodstream as we lounged around the hotel room prior to leaving. Then I remember LOSING MY MIND in the backseat of the car as we drove to the show. The next several hours were the worst eight hours of my entire life.

After staring out the car window for what seemed like four weeks, I mustered up the courage to say words.

"I need something to kick me out of this. I am starting to panic." I said turning to Jakie with eyes the size of planets. I needed vodka, a medical helicopter, or a gun to make it stop.

She gave me Adderall.

Now for those of you who do not know what Adderall is, ask any college student. The medical community claims it is an ADHD medication that can help you focus. I think it is crack cocaine soaked in LSD, cooked in meth, and topped off with anthrax and asbestos. I took it. Obviously.

Before we go any further in the story and closer to my impending death, let me explain a few things you should **never** do when you are overdosing on marijuana.

You should never:

- Speak.

- Look anyone in the eye.

- Tell your new friends how much you loved your dad who died when you were twenty-one.

- Go anywhere in public.

- Be around human beings.

- TAKE ADDERALL.

The Adderall kicked in as we pulled up to the festival, which forced me to focus 100 percent on my overwhelming paranoia. As a bonus, the medication intensified the "high" a few thousandfold and increased my blood pressure by infinity. Things were shaping up nicely. Hurray drugs.

If I had to guess, I would say we entered the festival, which was a massive polo ground, around four o'clock in the afternoon. I walked eighteen steps and sat down in the grass. And stared at my feet. For the next eight hours. I alternated between panic attacks and heart attacks every two minutes.

A few things I remember from my eight-hour sit-down were:

- Brad Pitt staring at me.

- Realizing it was not Brad Pitt.

- Thinking it was definitely Brad Pitt.

- Repeatedly telling myself "Marijuana **cannot** kill you."

- Repeatedly telling myself "Marijuana combined with Adderall **can** kill you."

- Thinking about standing up.

- Being too scared to stand up.

- Losing the feeling of my brain.

- Trying to remember to breathe.

- Wondering why thirty thousand festival goers were staring at me.

- Wondering when I would be able to verbally communicate with others.

- Wondering how many other forty-year-olds have died on weed at music festivals.

- Praying the paramedics would give me a hug.

- Trying yoga breathing exercises to bring my heart rate down from heart attack levels.

- Trying to explain to my friends we were all going to prison.

- The hippie girls looking at me like I was the dumbest human being they had ever met.

After seven hours, my friend Jakie, not her real name, finally convinced me to stand up, which was a terribly dangerous idea. I had not felt my legs in hours. I finally stood up and walked in the opposite direction of people. Away from the Brad Pitt who was not Brad Pitt.

"Let's go get a drink," Jakie, not her real name, suggested. She stuck by me the entire time. There was one problem…

To purchase a drink—and by purchase, I mean have her purchase because I was still terrified of human beings—I had to show my ID to the authorities. Two things that don't mix well are, first, authorities and second, weed overdoses.

Now, I can't even begin to explain to you how scary this was for me. I had to:

- Walk up to a table of human beings.

- Confidently determine which pocket held my ID.

- Seamlessly pull it out of my pocket without falling down.

- Avoid crying the whole time.

Thankfully, the effects of the marijuana faded after eight hours, which was the single greatest feeling of my life. I missed every single band at the festival but was still alive.

There were three things that saved my life that day. First, my friend Jakie—whose name is definitely not Jackie—who stayed by my side the entire day and loved me back to reality. Second, Brad Pitt. Well, not Brad Pitt. Third, laughter.

Jakie stuck by my side the entire day. She kept reassuring me I wasn't going to die. She hugged me when I needed hugs and distracted me when Brad Pitt was freaking me out. She was my rock.

The only consistent thing in my life that has helped me through the tough times has been laughter and good friends. I was blessed with the gift of humor, and it has been my saving grace. It has carried me through some dark times. Times when all I could do was laugh. Like my dumbass eating an entire weed brownie.

When we laugh together, we love together. We grow closer and are completely present in the moment. If we can inject a little more laughter into our lives, we get a little closer to love.

Jakie, not her real name, and I laugh about that day all the time now. Adventures that go South are sometimes the best stories we have. Assuming we don't die, which I surely almost did.

LOVE LESSONS

1. Laughter is the ultimate medicine, practice it daily. Go to comedy nights and regularly watch funny movies. Spend more time with your funny friends and less time with your unfunny friends. Laugh every day.

2. Be grateful for friends who stick with you through the challenging times. A good friend will be by your side when you lose your mind. We all lose our minds sometimes.

3. Never, ever, for the love of God, try marijuana.

17

FRANK'S LOVE LETTER

From the desk of FRANK SINATRA[7]

Chicken—a thought.

Strange, but I feel the world we live in demands that we be turned out in a pattern which resembles, in fact, a facsimile of itself. And those of us who roll with the punches, who grin, who dare to wear foolish clown faces, who defy the system—well, we do it, and bully for us!

Of course, there are those who do not. And the reason I think is that, (and I say this with some sadness) those up-tight, locked in people who resent and despise us, who fear us, and are bewildered by us, will one day come to realize that we possess rare and magical secrets, and more—love.

Therefore, I am beginning to think that a few, (I hope many) are wondering if maybe there might be value to a firefly, or an instant-long roman candle.

Keep the faith,
Dad

---

7   Nancy Sinatra, Legend: Frank Sinatra and the American Dream (Santa Monica: General Publishing Group, 1998), 13.

LOVE LESSONS

1. Celebrate your uniqueness. Don't compare your life to others. Shine bright, be weird.

2. Don't be the same as your neighbor. Wear colorful shoes and wild sunglasses.

3. Look for the magic in life and let it overwhelm you.

18

PREACHER AND POISON: PART 1

"Bananas are like love. You just have to find the one in the way it works for you—plain, on pancakes, in a drink, or fried."
    – JACK, SEVENTEEN YEARS OLD

A single fly. One single, annoying fly in the room. The damned thing landed on me every thirty-five seconds.

"Do you believe in ghosts?" I asked, trying to break the ice. I mentioned I was staying in town at the haunted hotel. Cody's eyebrows raised as he peered at me skeptically from his burgundy recliner. Cassy, his wife, was sitting on the floor with their infant baby.

One of the only hotels in town was the Historic Boone Tavern Hotel, which was built in 1907. It was listed as one of the top twenty-five most haunted hotels in America. My friend Ilene, who discovered the man I was about to inter-view, also found the hotel. We had driven several hours to a small, poor coal mining town in Kentucky to meet Cody.

The hotel was reportedly haunted so Ilene demanded they put me in the room most visited by ghosts. Of course, they gave me that room.

"I got you room 312." Ilene smirked.

"Why room 312?" I asked.

"It is the most haunted room in the hotel. They say the ghost of a little boy named Timmy is in that room," she told me with a shit-eating grin on her face.

Perfect. I was now in rural Kentucky to meet a snake-handling preacher while also staying in a hotel room with a ghost child. All for love.

Cody is a fourth-generation snake-handling preacher. His father died after being bitten by a snake during a church service. His sister was killed in a car accident. His life has been full of heartbreak to say the least.

"Y'all folla' us," Cody said from the passenger seat of a black SUV. We met him in the parking lot of a McDonald's after checking into the ghost hotel. His black SUV pulled out onto the main road and I followed behind. We drove along a two-lane road through the hills of Kentucky. Trump flags and abandoned shacks littered the side of the road. Eventually we turned onto a small, dirt road that led deep into the woods. I kept wondering why he wanted us to follow him to his house instead of just giving us the address. Following a man who plays with poisonous snakes to a strange house deep in the woods didn't seem like my smartest move.

"Text someone and let them know where we are in case we go missing." I shot a quick glance at Ilene.

We pulled up to his small house. They parked their car in front of mine and a woman got out of the driver side. Then he slowly got out of the passenger side. The preacher and his wife gave me a timid smile. Not too eager. I was surprised at how young they looked. Like two kids.

"Y'all come on in," he said in a soft, thick Southern accent, slowly making his way to the house. He was shorter and rounder than me. She was about his size. A small front porch ran along the front of the house. I noticed a white shed off to the left of the house, near the tree line. The kind of white shed you see in horror movies.

He sat in a burgundy recliner, so I sat next to him on a burgundy couch. His wife, Cassy, sat on a blanket on the floor with their newborn baby. It was a bit dark in the house. The floors and walls were made of dark wood. The room had very little furniture. Just a recliner, couch, and rug. It was spotless and organized.

Cody Coots has been bitten nine times by poisonous snakes. He has escaped death more times than he has fingers. His father died in his arms in the back of a Buick.

He was twenty-seven years old and his wife was twenty-three years old when I met them at their house. I was double those numbers.

"This is going to sound crazy," Cody said, answering my initial question about seeing ghosts. He had a soft, Southern voice.

Ilene quickly scrambled to press record on her phone. Anything that follows the phrase "this is going to sound crazy" usually will be pure gold. I stared at him, wondering what he was about to tell me.

"I definitely believe in ghosts. I was possessed by a demon named Nina." His eyes got wider as he looked at me for the first time.

I was speechless. Ilene was speechless. The baby was speechless. Cody stared at me. His wife stared at me. I nodded my head as I gathered my thoughts.

"Really?" I asked, attempting to remain calm and casual as one does after someone tells you they have been possessed by a demon named Nina.

"Yeah. For about a year. I was in a bad spot. I was a different person. It was awful," Cody mumbled and looked back down at his wife on the floor. He continuously rocked back and forth in the recliner.

"I didn't even recognize his face," Cassy said as the baby, possibly possessed, tussled in her arms.

Cody and Cassy started debating when the possession happened and for how long. He talked about hating God, wanting to kill himself and others, and leading a very destructive life while possessed. Neither Cody nor Cassy were showboating or boasting about any of this. His body language told a story of shame and embarrassment.

Cody looked over at me and said, "I have held a gun to my head, her head, and wanted to shoot people in the church. I was picking up prostitutes every week and was addicted to porn while trying to keep my first marriage going for fear of being blackballed by the church if I got divorced. I was the preacher at the time because when my dad died, they forced me to take his spot. It was awful. I was lost."

My first thought: Why am I in a house with a guy who wanted to shoot people?

My second thought: Why am I in a house with a guy who wanted to shoot people and was possessed by a demon named Nina?

Oddly enough, Cody was growing on me. The way he talked, slowly and thoughtfully, and the stories he told had a feeling of authenticity. He didn't speak much and stared at his wife most of the time.

Cassy spoke more than he did. She was more animated and engaged in the conversation with us and had a "can you believe that" tone when she spoke. A feeling of pain, really. We just met, but it felt like I had known her much longer.

"Does anybody get bit?" I asked Cody, shifting away from demons and murderous thoughts to snake bites.

"That is the most common question I get asked," he laughed softly. "I been bitten nine times. Nine, right?" He looked to his wife for confirmation.

"Yes, nine times. His daddy was bit ten times. The tenth killed him. That's why I worry 'bout his next bite." Cassy gave Cody the evil eye, like a mother disappointed in her child. The baby squirmed in her arms.

"Does it hurt?" I asked like an idiot. Does a bite from a poisonous snake hurt? I am a horrible journalist. Clearly.

"That rattlesnake bite hurt the worst. Like a hammer pounding on my hand." Cody made the motion of a hammer as he looked at his hand to show me the scar.

Handling poisonous snakes, or taking up serpents, arose from the Pentecostal Church. An article from ABC News which covered Cody's father's death wrote:

"It's estimated that 125 churches in the United States use poisonous snakes during services today, with many clustered in the South. In tiny churches tucked away in rural Appalachia, 'snake handling' is a long-standing tradition, one that took root in this region more than a century ago. These pastors believe that to 'take up serpents' is a form of religious expression. The King James Bible, Mark 16:18 says, 'They shall take up serpents; and if they drink any deadly thing, it shall not hurt them.'"[8]

---

8   Spencer Wilking and Lauren Effron, "Snake-Handling Pentecostal Pastor Dies From Snake Bite," ABC News, February 17, 2014.

Cody's family is well-known because MTV filmed a documentary about him and his church. They caught him getting bitten on the head by a rattlesnake during the filming.

"That bite about took me out," he explained. "It was a black rattlesnake and got me right on the head. I couldn't walk in twenty minutes, so I said take me home and let me die. My buddy, Big Cody, said 'I ain't gonna let you die. We lost your Paw Paw, and I ain't gonna let you die. So you can go to the hospital right now or I am going to take you when you black out from the poison.'"

Cody was oddly nonchalant when talking about the snake bites. Except this one. He looked genuinely scared as he told us about it.

"When we was at the hospital I asked the doctor, 'do you think you will be able to save me?' I was scared to death, man. My throat was closing. The doctor asked, 'do you promise to quit handling them snakes?' and I said 'no, let me die.' The doctor turned and walked out of the room, and I coded. My heart stopped and they shocked me back and induced a coma. I woke up ten days later." His eyes were big and scared.

I kept thinking this guy really is not scared of dying. I was glued to every word. Everything he said fascinated me. I also wondered what the hell Ilene was thinking. She was Jewish and was probably thinking Christianity was nothing more than a serpent-holding cult full of demons and weirdos.

Cody told me about the other snake bites, being raised in a strict church, and how jobs were hard to find. He caught, traded, and sold snakes to support his family after he was fired from his regular job because a snake bite kept him out of work for a few days.

My heart hurt for them. I tried to imagine how hard it would be growing up in a small town in a strict religious environment with little to no money. Cassy got married for the first time when she was sixteen years old. Her first husband abused and controlled her. She started drinking every day and was an alcoholic by the time she was eighteen. Cody was married at nineteen years old because his father, the head of the church at the time, threatened to kick him out of church and home if he didn't change his ways. He was a teenage boy doing normal, teenage boy things.

"I never should have married the first time. I just did it because that is what we do in the church. We have to marry in order to have relations," he sighed.

"What is your definition of love?" I launched into my love questions.

Cody paused and looked up at the ceiling as he kept rocking in his recliner. "Well, I love the Lord, but my favorite love story is my true love for her." He motioned his head toward his wife. His face relaxed, and the edges of his mouth turned into a smile. His entire demeanor shifted. "When I fell in love with her, it was different. True love changed me from picking up prostitutes and watching porn and all those things. So when I got with her, I did not desire them things anymore. Ain't no one else as beautiful as she is. She is perfect. I never thought I could find love again because with my first wife, I was a bad person."

Cody met Cassy in the church he was leading after his father's death. He was lost, she was lost, and two desperate souls collided to heal each other.

"Do you love yourself?" I asked.

In a soft voice he replied, "Yeah, yeah I do." He paused. "I love who I am now. I hate who I was then."

Interesting, I thought. It reminded me we can change. Here was a twenty-seven-year-old man who had been to the gates of hell reminding me we can find love, peace, and new beginnings. Cody had lost his father, sister, wife, church, and soul, yet somehow, against all odds, he found himself again.

"What is the hardest thing that ever happened to you?" I asked, assuming his father's death or maybe one of the snake bites had been the worst.

"Getting molested." He looked up.

Startled by his answer, I asked, "Was it someone in your family?"

"Naw, someone from the church." He kept rocking.

I looked down at Cassy on the floor, not knowing what to say next. She looked at me and said, "I was molested and raped by my family members."

Damn, I thought. The hits just kept on coming. My heart continued to ache for both Cody and his wife. I looked at the baby and wondered what kind of world he was going to grow up in. I wondered if he would ever meet his dad, the man next to me, before something tragic happened.

The sun was setting and I didn't want us to overstay our welcome. They had been extremely vulnerable and open with us. We had been talking for a couple of hours, and it really did feel like we were all family at that point. It is hard not to love someone when you hear their real story.

Toward the end of our conversation I asked, "Are you afraid of dying?"

"No, I am not afraid of dying. I know where I am going when I die," Cody said confidently. Then he added, "I know I won't make it to fifty years old though."

The odd thing about him saying that was I believed him. He wasn't being funny. He honestly believed it.

"No sir, you are going to live to over a hundred!" I smiled.

As we drove back to the hotel, I couldn't stop thinking about our conversation with Cody and his wife Cassy. I had never heard such stories of pain and perseverance in my life. I was awestruck at how such young people had lived long lives already. It also gave me hope for my life and my lifelong quest to find love. It seemed like those two lost souls were able to find love…to love themselves and each other. I was looking forward to joining them at their church service the next day. I had no idea what to expect…

LOVE LESSONS

1. Love doesn't care about your past. Love can happen at any time to anyone. Past hardships, abuse, and broken hearts do not prevent us from loving fully now and in the future. There is always hope. Let's open our hearts.

2. Everyone can change. We all have our demons. However, we can overcome our demons and live a happy, fulfilling life full of love if we so choose. We change once we decide we must change.

3. The diamondback rattlesnake bite hurts the worst. Cody told me, "Your legs go numb and your hands get ice-cold. It is the worst pain in the entire world. You get a tingly feeling in your tongue, and that's when you know you are in bad shape."

19

PREACHER & POISON: PART 2

———

"Bananas are love because my dog loves bananas, and I love my dog."

— JORDAN, NINE YEARS OLD

The next morning, Cody and Cassy met us at Cracker Barrel for breakfast. I offered to buy them breakfast before the church service.

"Sure, I love food," Cody replied when I asked the night before.

Ilene and I arrived first and got a small table for four. Cody arrived and lumbered to our table. He was carrying a car seat with the baby. Cassy, his wife, was by his side. She was in a proper dress, the kind you might see Amish women wear. Traditional. He wore a vest and slacks. Church clothes, as we used to call them growing up.

Cody ordered biscuits and gravy with a Mello Yello. Cassy ordered eggs and bacon with water. She was trying to lose her baby weight on the keto diet. Cody casually fed the baby some of his biscuit as we made small talk over breakfast. I wondered if babies eat biscuits. I got my answer a few moments later when the baby started choking and threw up.

"Do something." Cassy poked Cody in the arm. The baby was next to him and not her.

He looked at her and nodded. Then he casually took a straw, dipped it in his Mello Yello, and fed it to the baby. I wondered if babies drink Mello Yello. The baby promptly vomited, again.

After breakfast, we followed them to Middlesboro, Kentucky, where his grandfather and mother lived. It was also the town of his family's church. We arrived at his grandfather's house to gather up some snakes from the shed. As Cody went to get the snakes, I walked inside the house to meet his mom and Paw Paw. The first thing I noticed was a gigantic snake in a box with a clear lid sitting on the end table next to the couch.

It was a small brick house. Very clean. Paw Paw was a short man. We shook hands. No words were exchanged. Mom was about his size with long, gray hair. I said hello as she sat patiently on the couch, an arm's length from the snake box.

Cody loaded some snake boxes into his car and we headed to the church. It was a tiny, windowless building on the side of a hill. Five or six cars sat in the lopsided, gravel parking lot. Ilene and I entered and took a seat in the third row. There were a few people scattered around the room.

It was a small, one-room church about the size of a basketball court. Wood floors, wood walls, wood pews. A few odd pictures hung on the walls.

I counted nine instruments, seven boxes full of poisonous snakes, and twenty-four people in the room. The crowd was older. Cody's grandfather took his position behind the pulpit. He looked like an older Robert De Niro. White hair, thick chest, serious face. A man of few words. A man who looked like he had seen a few things in his life.

A few more folks wandered into the church as Cody's grandfather started the service.

"Please pray for Mary who just got out of rehab. Pray she can find her way again," a lady from the back called out.

"I'd like to pray for Paul who is havin' a time finding the Lord," a man yelled out.

Eventually Paw Paw finished the prayer round and picked up his acoustic guitar. The others on stage—I counted seven people—grabbed their instruments.

A young woman in a conservative dress with brown hair piled into a messy bun on top of her head got up and walked to a microphone near the pulpit. She began to sing. All the musical instruments slowly followed her lead. She sang, cried, and sang some more. Cody's mother played a drum set in the corner. Her long, gray hair was piled into a bun as well. She wore an oversized, monogrammed, long-sleeve, tie-dye shirt with a long skirt and no shoes.

A tall, young, cowboy-looking dude stood in the corner wearing a red Western shirt tucked into black jeans. His hair was tight and organized, razor short on the sides and flat on the top. He had an electric guitar in his hands. Cody stood next to him playing an electric bass. Paw Paw played an acoustic guitar. A guest preacher sat in a chair behind the pulpit playing an acoustic guitar. Cody's wife also played an acoustic guitar. There were more guitars than humans. A handful of tambourines and a set of cymbals worked their way to members sitting in the pews. Pure, full-blown gospel rock and roll filled the tiny room. It. Was. Amazing.

At the end of each song, a guy in the row across from me would holler, "Praise Jesus," and the instruments would slowly wind down to silence. Then, as if the Holy Spirit tapped them on the shoulder, someone would inevitably walk up to the microphone and start singing the next song. I couldn't tell if they were making up songs or singing ones they knew. I also couldn't tell what in the hell was going on at any given point, but I loved every second of it. The music was rattling my bones.

Cody moved to the drums as another woman took over the microphone. She poured all of her suffering into her song. People moved around the front of the room like wandering ants. It was chaos.

At one point, a young man from the front row stood up and raised his hands toward the sky. I kept my eye on him because he had arrived earlier with a big box of snakes. He moved to the music. Not much though, just slightly shifting his shoulders side to side with his eyes closed. After a few moments, he lowered his hands to one of the snake boxes. Showtime.

He opened the box, reached in, and pulled out four rattlesnakes. Two in each hand. He held them up above his head. Chris, a balding, slightly overweight man, pulled a small rope from the corner of the first pew across the aisle to the corner of the opposite pew. I suppose it was to keep people from walking into the snakes' den. I noticed a sign on the wall when I arrived that said, "No one under eighteen years old allowed to hold serpents." Rules are rules.

Two kids in the row in front of me pounded on tambourines. Several women stood in the front, stomping on the floor. The man raised the snakes above his head.

After a few moments, he passed the snakes to Paw Paw who raised them to the sky and then passed them to the preacher. Then to Cody. Then they handed them to Cody's mother.

Cody's mom was now holding four rattlesnakes. It had to be one of the most interesting things I have ever seen in my life. Well, until she picked up a bottle of fire.

She handed the snakes back to one of the men as the cowboy-shirt guy handed her a glass bottle with a rag hanging out of the top. He lit the damn thing on fire, and then Cody's mom passed fire over her throat and hands. While dancing. Barefoot.

I have seen a lot of wild things in my life, but this took the cake. It was mesmerizing, confusing, and seemingly dangerous. All in the name of the Lord. I couldn't help but wonder what Ilene was thinking about all of this. Clearly, she has never experienced anything like this being raised in a Jewish household. I shot a glance at her and noticed her eyes were glued on the snakes. She inched closer to me.

The hoopla carried on for about an hour. They spoke in tongues and sweated through their shirts. They celebrated, wailed, cried, and danced. It was fantastic.

There was some serious spirit in that room.

Eventually, the music died down, and the guest preacher took to the pulpit. He ranted and raved about everything for around an hour. No notes, no script, just preaching whatever came to his mind in a paced, rhythmic fashion. He would shout, pause, wipe his brow with a handkerchief, and shout some more.

"Come on!" a man from the third row shouted. "Tell 'em, Brother Earl," a woman behind me called out. I didn't say a word.

Eventually, the preacher turned it back over to Paw Paw to conclude the service. The room died down as Paw Paw slumped over the pulpit, resting his arm on the top as if he'd just ran a marathon at eighty years old. He mumbled something and waited for members to speak up.

A few members stood up and gave thanks for the service and asked for prayers. The last one to speak was Cody's mom from the back of the room.

"I want to thank God for the opportunity to worship and be with each of you today. I want to thank God for moving me to hold serpents today. It has been over a month since I have held serpents," she said, looking around the room. "We don't hold serpents to see if they bite or for show. We hold them because of how it makes us feel inside, in our souls. We hold them to feel how powerful we all are, and as a reminder that love is the most important feeling in the world."

Amen girl.

As I sat in the pew, I thought about spirituality. What it means, how we find it, and why it is important. I thought about how the root word of spirituality is spirit. And what is spirit? A feeling? Energy? Love?

A spirit engulfed that room, those people, and me. It was moving, filled with joy, relief, and hope. I felt connected to all the people in the room. Connected to the music, the pain, and the stories they told. I felt the spirit inside me wake up and dance.

I don't know whether it is right or wrong to hold snakes, speak in tongues, or believe we all have the power to heal others. I think rituals do bring us closer to love, God, and each other though. The service was one of the most beautiful experiences of my life. I am grateful for those people and those snakes.

LOVE LESSONS

1. When each person entered the church before the service, they walked up to everybody in the room, including me and Ilene, and shook their hands. Then they would move to the next person. No words, no small talk; just shake and move. I found this very interesting. A ritual that forced connection with each person. I think we should always engage everyone in the room before we start meetings, dinners, or other gatherings. This was a great lesson for me.

2. During the service, as one member would be singing, holding the snakes, or speaking in tongues, others would place a hand on the person's back. This, as I was told later, was because they believed they had the power to heal each other. I too believe we have the power to heal each other if we lend a hand or offer a comforting pat on the back. Physical touch is a powerful form of kindness, care, and love.

3. Handle snakes at your own risk.

20

HUGS IN BALI

"You need a lot of water for bananas to grow so love is kind of like a tree that has to be nurtured."

– ELLIE, THIRTEEN YEARS OLD

I drove my illegally rented scooter to the orphanage. I should have taken a taxi to make sure I found the place, but the roads in Bali are skinny, winding, and a huge pain in the ass. The only way to reasonably get anywhere is by scooter. Google Maps said it was a thirty-minute drive. It took me two-and-a-half hours. The map on my phone stopped working two minutes into my journey. Every turn was a guess. Every street was a mess. That rhymed.

I was spending three weeks in Bali, Indonesia, on my continued quest to discover love. Yoga, sunshine, beaches, and organic everything. A real soul cleanse to open my heart and clean my chakras. I have no idea what chakras are, but they might as well be cleaned.

I was on my way to an orphanage that was run by a man who had rescued thousands of children over the years. My buddy Garrett suggested I reach out to this man.

"His story is amazing, and if there is anyone who is good at love, it is this guy!" Garrett insisted when he found out I was headed to Bali.

"Really?" My ears perked up.

"Yeah, he was running an orphanage and got a tip that religious extremists were burning down villages, orphanages, and places of worship that were non-Muslim. He had over one hundred kids in his care and less than an hour to make a decision!"

"What happened?" I asked looking up from my computer where I was researching flights to Bali.

"His orphanage was in-between the ocean and the jungle. He decided to wake up all the kids in the middle of the night and head high into the jungle. He got them all out and could see his orphanage burn to the ground below. In the chaos, he realized his own daughter was missing, so he panicked. Against all odds, he went back toward the burning orphanage and found her crying in a riverbed that she fell into in the attempt to escape," Garrett passionately told me.

"Holy shit."

He said, "At that moment I realized that God saved her life, and I wanted to dedicate my life to saving others."

My scooter bounced along the road into the capital city of Denpasar. I was staying in the beach town of Canggu which is full of digital nomads spending their dad's money and amateur surfers taking Instagram photos.

Scooters weaved in and out of gridlock traffic while fruit carts and pedestrians clogged up the streets. My eyes darted from left to right trying to avoid getting smashed by a truck or launched into a ditch full of town garbage. Leathery men aged by the sun and a lifetime of labor struggled behind flatbed carts carrying bricks and wooden boards. People swarmed around open-air shops selling everything from socks to mops. Traffic rules be damned.

The man who started the orphanage was out of town, but his wife was there. Women are smarter than men, so I was happy to go anyway.

I arrived at the orphanage wet as a mop from sweat and panic. The heat index in Bali was volcanic. I parked my scooter, toweled off as best I could, and entered a white building, praying for air conditioning and all the answers to love. A high-energy gal named Marliesye greeted me at once. She had a smile as wide as the ocean and big, brown eyes. My face was still sweating.

"Hi there! You must be Trey!" she announced with open arms.

"Yes ma—" I mumbled as she pulled me in for a hug. Fair enough. We hug now.

She was gorgeous. Long brown hair and silky smooth, dark skin. She mentioned she was thirty-five years old. She looked twenty-five. Stunning.

I followed her upstairs to her office and sat in a chair facing her desk. Her office was small but had air conditioning. God shined his light on me.

A young Indonesian girl with perfect posture stood near the door in a light blue school uniform with her arms behind her back. She was a teenage orphan Marliesye took under her wing years ago. The young girl's entire family died in an uprising on one of the islands in Indonesia. Her smile was outstanding and grateful. At twelve years of age, she had worked her way up to being Marliesye's assistant. She looked proud of it too.

Marliesye and her husband had been rescuing orphans for over twenty years throughout Indonesia. They saved hundreds of children, most of who have gone on to find successful jobs and start their own families.

"What is love?" I asked, kicking things off.

She looked at me like I was nuts. I blindsided her with the love question. It blindsides everyone. Try it sometime. Try it every time.

She looked up, thought for a moment, and then asked me, "Well, what do you think it is?"

What? Nobody turns my questions back on me. Panic. I had no idea. Now I was going to look like an idiot. An idiot sweating through his pants. "I don't know. I am writing a book about it," I deflected. I am an expert in deflecting.

She smiled. She had a warmness about her.

"We find children lost in the streets, sometimes alone after their parents have been killed in civil unrest," she explained to me with a soft heart. "We find kids wandering in the streets or woods after their entire village is destroyed by violence. No parents, no food, and nowhere to go. We take them in," she continued to explain. "The kids have nowhere to go, no one to help them, and nothing to eat," she said frowning.

That is rough. I couldn't imagine a tsunami or political violence wiping out my entire family in an instant. How horrible for anybody, much less children.

She also explained the difficulty of being a Christian-based organization in a Muslim-dominated country. Indonesia, comprised of 17,508 islands and around 239 million people, is 87.2 percent Muslim and 9.9 percent Christian.[9] Raising money and resources has always been challenging for her and the orphanage because of their

---

9 "The Future of World Religions: Population Growth Projections, 2010-2050," Pew Research Center, Washington, D.C., April 2, 2015.

religious affiliation to a minority. Most of the donations come from churches around the world. A threat of violence always hovers around non-Muslim organizations. All together it makes it challenging for them to keep the orphanage going each year.

She had a sparkle in her eye. I loved her energy. Not only was she very attractive, she was charming too.

"I am actually fifty-three, not thirty-five, but I like to reverse the numbers." She winked and laughed.

Damn, I thought. Fooled me.

"Love is a hug." She smiled.

"A hug?" I replied curiously.

While most people I asked tried to come up with a long, intellectual answer for the definition of love, she simply said it was a hug.

"Yes, a hug. When I find kids who have been abandoned and lost after a tsunami or violence, I just give them a hug. That's it. I don't talk to them. I don't tell them everything is going to be okay. I don't want them to love me back. I just give them a hug." She sat back in her chair.

I have never liked hugs. My dad never hugged me, and I would usually squirm to escape all hugs from other adults. The more I think about it, I might have a severe hug deficit. I live alone, don't hug dudes, and barely see my mom. I wonder if people, families, or couples who hug regularly are better at love and happier. My guess is yes.

Virginia Satir, a popular family therapist, states, "We need four hugs a day for survival. We need eight hugs a day for maintenance. We need twelve hugs a day for growth."[10]

---

10   Erica Cirino, "What Are the Benefits of Hugging," Healthline, April 10, 2018.

An article on Healthline suggests the following seven benefits of hugging:

1. Hugs reduce stress by showing your support.

2. Hugs may protect you against illness.

3. Hugs may boost your heart health.

4. Hugs can make you happier.

5. Hugs help reduce your fears.

6. Hugs may help reduce your pain.

7. Hugs help you communicate with others.[11]

Science geeks report hugs release oxytocin, the happiness and bonding hormone. As such, hugging people would make happier people. I was at a love intensive retreat recently where the head therapist told us it takes twenty-one seconds for oxytocin to be released during a hug. That is a long hug for an amateur hugger like me. It would be hell to get through the first twenty seconds. I have some work to do.

"What do the kids usually do when you hug them?" I asked Marliesye, wondering how they react.

"Most of them hug me back."

---

11 Ibid.

LOVE LESSONS

1. Set a goal for eight hugs a day, or if you are like me, one hug a day. Baby steps. Make it your mission to become a master hugger and don't be worried what other people think.

2. I dare you to ask for a hug from a stranger. Do it three times today and see what happens.

3. If you rent a scooter in Bali, make sure you have good traveler's health insurance.

21

THE TERRIFYING TEA

———

Love feeds life and so does the banana."

— MELISSA, ELEVEN YEARS OLD

"Do you have any last-minute questions?" Jasmine asked in a soft voice from the bed across from me. A little man was sitting next to her. She was pregnant. Maybe his, maybe not.

I was in a dark room in a strange house. The little man she called "Poppo" sat motionless next to her and spoke no English. Really didn't speak at all. Just smiled. They stared at me. My hands were shaking. Not enough for them to notice though.

"Am I going to die?" I asked for the millionth time.

"No," she said with a reassuring smile. "However, once you are in it, you are in it and there is no getting out." Poppo raised his eyebrows as if he understood what she said. He didn't. He didn't speak English. He sat on the bed with his legs twisted under him like a yogi. His hair was jet black and gathered in a ponytail that ran down his back. The front half of his head was shaved like if you cut a watermelon in half.

Front half, no hair. Back half, long hair. It was a bizarre look but made me feel better for some reason. Like he knew what he was doing. I clearly didn't.

If adventure requires uncertainty about the outcome, well, by God, this was going to be an adventure.

Jasmine had convinced me to do three ceremonies over the course of three nights. My hope was to get a better understanding of love. Perhaps find some answers on why love had been so hard for me. Over the next three nights I would discover an alien, dance with rainbow crickets, and see the blueprint of my soul. Oh, and I saw God. That was bananas.

I have never been a spiritual guy. Growing up, I was spoon-fed Christianity as my grandparents hauled me into their small churches and my mom took us to a few others. However, nothing was ever consistent. Then, as I started traveling the world, I discovered different cultures, religions, and beliefs. Now in this season of my life, I am starting to explore spirituality. There just might be something beyond us pulling a few of the strings.

One time I sat on the steps of a massive Catholic cathedral in Mexico City with a local man who told me how the Spanish came and destroyed all the Aztec temples in his city. I have attended a Buddhist funeral in rural Thailand and had coffee with a Voodoo priest in Benin, Africa. Muslims invited me to pray with them in Sudan, and I interviewed a pet psychic in Atlanta, but never experienced anything like what was about to happen.

The house had two bedrooms and loads of hippie, new age wall hangings. Dream catchers, bamboo sticks with beads, and bizarre posters of hieroglyphics. It was your standard woo-woo house owned by your standard woo-woo dude; rope necklace, long ponytail, calming voice, weird pants.

"What is your intention for the ceremony?" Jasmine calmly asked. She had long, beautiful black hair and golden-brown skin.

"To try and understand love." I replied, almost embarrassed. A grown man trying to figure out love in a bizarre house with bizarre people.

She smiled. Poppo smiled. I didn't smile.

"Okay, let's go." She stood up from the bed and a lightning bolt of fear shot through my body. Am I really going to do this?

We moved to the main room of the house. I sat down on my sleeping bag laid out on the floor. A guy next to me sat on his sleeping bag. Jasmine and Poppo settled in the front of the room. The ceremony was about to begin.

Poppo starting chanting in a language foreign to me. He raised his hands to the sky and shifted his body left to right. A prayer to the gods, I supposed. The ceremony began.

Poppo was a shaman from Peru. He came from a long lineage of shamans. I was told he had been performing these ceremonies since he was seventeen years old. That was twenty-three years ago.

"Come up." Jasmine motioned toward me with her hands. The room was dark, lit only by a single candle. Looming really.

I crawled from my sleeping bag to the shaman. My heart was racing as he poured a black liquid into a very small cup and handed it to me.

"Drink," he said, using the only word he knew in English. His eyes caught mine, and I said a silent prayer to the universe.

I drank the juice. It tasted like death. A rank, earthy, bile-tasting sludge.

I crawled back to my sleeping bag and laid down on my back. A bucket had been placed beside me for vomit. The candle was blown out, and we waited in darkness.

Thirty long minutes later, the shaman started playing music with instruments he brought from his home in Peru. The medicine started kicking in, and I could feel my heart start racing. My right leg started kicking up and down for no reason. Things were getting weird.

Suddenly my chest tightened, I started to hyperventilate, and broke out in a cold sweat. I was confident I was dying of a full-blown heart attack. Panic consumed my entire body and I shot up to a seated position, gasping for a breath. My face was covered in sweat as my mind began to bend, tangle, and jumble into a mess. The shaman shuffled over to me. He sat right in front of me, his face inches from mine, and started chanting. He grabbed both sides of my head with his hands and started bobbed his head left and right while chanting in each of my ears. He blew smoke in my face from a pipe he was smoking and massaged oil on the back of my neck. I was so confused as to what he was doing it pulled me out of my anxiety attack. He was able to bring me into a trance where I focused on him instead of my impeding death. A few moments later, I was peacefully lying on my mat. Still alive. The odd, little Peruvian man saved my life.

Then, I blasted off into the universe.

This, my friends, was my first ayahuasca ceremony. An article on Medical News Today states ayahuasca is a psychoactive tea people, mainly in the Amazon, make using the leaves of the *Psychotria viridis* plant and the stalks of the *Banisteriopsis caapi* vine. Both plant ingredients in ayahuasca tea have hallucinogenic properties. The leaves of the *P. viridis* plant contain N,N-dimethyltryptamine (DMT), which is a strong psychedelic compound. "People in Ecuador, Colombia, Peru, and Brazil have used ayahuasca as a healing medicine or as part of religious ceremonies or tribal rituals for thousands of years."[12]

Well, it tastes like vomit and launches you into outer space for eight hours.

The shaman continued to chant, sing, and fart over the next several hours. The room filled with smoke from his special tobacco, and I floated in and out of a dream-like state. The medicine gave me a front row seat to all my past traumas. It was like watching the movie of my life right before my eyes.

For example, at one point, a looming voice from the universe said, "This is why you are so lonely," and showed me crying when I was eleven years old during an experience where my mother and I were on vacation. She left me in the hotel room while she went to dinner with friends. Land crabs kept trying to get in the room, scratching at the door, and I was terrified.

A couple of hours into my experience, an alien appeared right before my eyes. It had a huge head and massive, pitch-black eyes. We stared at each other. No words were spoken yet I could sense what he, she, or it was thinking. It had no mouth. As we locked eyes, it felt like the damn thing was hugging me. Then it was gone. A full-blown alien.

At one point, I looked over at the shaman. He turned into a massive bald eagle. Then I was sitting in a field with Jesus. Next, I was flying through the universe. Oh, and I saw the light of God which was too powerful to look at directly.

The brew was working, obviously.

Five hours later, the shaman closed the ceremony and went into the kitchen with Jasmine and Joel Darby, the dude

---

12 Jayne Leonard, "What to Know about Ayahuasca," Medical News Today, January 31, 2020, accessed April 23, 2020.

who was next to me. They brought me a banana, and I laughed because I thought I was a gorilla. Literally. The ayahuasca wore off, and I fell asleep right there on my sleeping bag.

The next morning, I woke up and realized:

1. I had to repeat the ceremony two more times.

2. There was no way I could repeat the ceremony two more times.

I contemplated leaving all morning. Should I tell them I am done, or stay and do two more nights? The first night was long, hard, and intense. However, I had paid for them, and I am a cheap bastard, so I decided to stay. I would rather die than lose one hundred dollars, which was a fair possibility given the insanity that happened the first night.

We started at nine o'clock the second night. I nervously drank the medicine and moved back onto my sleeping bag. Two new people, a gigantic man named Tim Carlson and a psychic woman named Jennifer Lester, joined the ceremony. As we blasted into the universe, the gigantic man fell sound asleep, and the woman started crying hysterically. Round two.

The second ceremony would prove to be different. Instead of pain and darkness, it showed me every positive experience of my life: winning the National Championship in college as a mascot, girls I've loved, family, and all the joys of my past. At one point, I was dancing in a field of yellow flowers with hundreds of people off in the distance cheering me on. They were clapping and shouting for me. Some looked like dead relatives and others ancient ancestors. When I stopped dancing, the entire sky closed in around me as they all said, "We will see you again," and vanished. Thinking back, if there is such thing as heaven, that was it. I have never felt more accepted and supported in my life.

Toward the end of the night, someone started playing a piano in the corner of the room. The second I heard the notes float off the piano keys, tears blasted from my eyes. I was instantly in a dream, sitting next to my father on a piano bench.

"Dad?" I looked up at him. He smiled and looked at me as his fingers danced across the piano. He looked happy, healthy, and excited to see me.

"I love you." His eyes met mine. My heart melted. This time, it felt real.

"I love you. I miss you. Why, Dad?" I asked. I don't think there is an answer to a question that big. Why did he die on me? Why did he choose the bottle over me? Why did he let me down a million times? Why did he attack me when I was younger?

"I will be sorry forever. I let you down and was not a good father. You deserved the world, and I was not able to give it to you. I am sorry." Tears trickled down his face.

It was an honest answer. One I had been wanting my whole life.

In the end, we hugged. It was a hug unlike any I had ever felt in my life.

"I love you. Everything is okay now." He finished. And it was. And it is.

I don't remember much from the third night of ceremonies, but I will always remember being at the piano with my father. A moment and a conversation forty years in the making. A healing I so desperately wanted my entire life.

I forgive you, Dad. I love you. You did your best, and I know you loved me. Everything is okay now.

Was it real? Was I just dreaming on drugs? It doesn't matter to me. In my heart, I can still feel the love from that night on that bench next to my father. I can still feel the love I sent to my friends and family during my experience. I can still feel the love of God, too blinding to see.

Love is an adventure. Sometimes we find it in the oddest places. A small shaman from the jungles of Peru guided me through an experience of a lifetime. A mysterious brew of bark and vine opened my heart, showed me God, and let me love my dad again. In the end, I got a taste of the perfect love.

Oh, I took a few notes at the end of each ceremony to remember the madness. I thought you might enjoy a good laugh...

Day 1
- Seeing God.
- Hugging dad, feeling his neck.
- Peeing in toilet.
- Saying "I love you" in their eyes.
- Shaman danced over me.
- Blue balls of energy.
- FUCKING great.
- Hand on heart.
- Tapping chest.
- Monkey eating banana.
- Shaman singing into universe.
- I made it.
- Guy next to me different masks.
- Farting.
- Shaman purging.
- Singing to me close to him.
- Bliss.

Day 2
- Meet an alien with black eye.
- Rainbow crickets.
- The heartbeat of my dead dog.
- Sitting with dad at piano.
- Sarah kiss into cosmos.
- Family with blue feathers.
- Kissing Chris's head.
- Billy's unborn child.

LOVE LESSONS

1. A lack of forgiveness turns our hearts black. We must forgive others to love fully. We don't have to forget, just forgive. It is for us, not them. I forgave my father while sitting at the piano bench, and now I can feel his love.

2. Resistance destroys us. My resistance to the experience created panic attacks the first night. When I finally let go, the medicine took me to magical places. Love is like that too. The longer I resist it, the harder it becomes. I needed to make an effort to accept love instead of deflecting and resisting it. Open hearts practice acceptance over resistance.

3. Never try ayahuasca without a trusted, proven, experienced, safe, legit, honest, loving shaman. When the wheels come off—and the wheels will definitely come off—you want a pro in your corner. Someone who has handled that very situation a thousand times.

22

THIRTY-DAY LIST

———

I was mind-numbingly bored a few years ago. I was in a rut, fighting depression, and aggravated at how lame my life had become. Love? Not even close. I needed to figure out a way to kick-start my life again. On a whim, I sat down and wrote thirty things I had always been curious about or scared to try. Then, like a weirdo, I decided to try and do them all in thirty days. I posted the list on Facebook to hold myself accountable. It transformed my life.

What is so magical about this list? I'm glad you asked.

It forced me to do something! I needed to quit reading books and hiding in my condo. I needed to try new things, get uncomfortable, and push through fears. I needed to get unstuck.

HERE IS MY FIRST THIRTY-DAY LIST:
1. Take a sound bath class.
2. Memorize a poem.
3. Write thirty blogs in thirty days.
4. Cook soup.
5. Try Jiu-Jitsu class.
6. Get a Brazilian wax.

7. Spend three hours at an old folks' home.
8. Go to a drum circle.
9. Write an outline for a book.
10. Take mushrooms in nature.
11. Pet a horse.
12. Do a three-day fast.
13. Start a book club.
14. Go to Creflo Dollar's church.
15. Create a piece of art and sell it.
16. Get one coaching client.
17. Mail letters to ten people.
18. Take a Kundalini yoga class.
19. Give a speech.
20. Record one podcast.
21. Try acupuncture.
22. Get a meditation certification.
23. Try LSD.
24. Sell my couch.
25. Give blood.
26. Go on a date.
27. Take a breathwork class.
28. Read a book about love.
29. Do a five-minute stand-up comedy set.
30. Throw a dinner party.

I finished twenty-seven of the thirty things on my list. Not bad. I was turned down when trying to give blood, and I never pet a horse. The book club never took off. Enough about me. Let's talk about you.

Hey, reader of my book—take action.

PICK ONE THING FROM MY LIST ABOVE AND DO IT IN THE NEXT TWENTY-FOUR HOURS.

If you only get one thing from this book, it is this...try new things, have fun, get scared. I guess that was technically three. Whatever. Pick one thing from the list above that makes you nervous and go do it in the next twenty-four hours. Tag me on twitter or Instagram @treygoesglobal and use hashtag #loveisbananas when you do, or we are no longer besties. Love is an action, not a theory.

If you want help creating your very own Thirty-Day List, email me trey@iamtrey.com!

3

LOVE IS TOTALLY WORTH IT

23

LET'S FIND LOVE

———

The first kiss. Sex in the rain. A best friend like Lester, a desert road in Yemen, or the psychiatric ward in San Francisco. Love is as boundless as bananas. She can have twenty-five orgasms in a row, he can manifest a lover, and she is a witch without a broom. Perhaps these folks can teach us how to find love because it is totally worth it!

24

DYING FOR SEX

"If you break a banana it is never the same, so is love, so be careful not to break it."

— KELVIN, SIX YEARS OLD

I sat in my car with tears running down my face. The girl I was dating texted me and asked what I was doing. I typed, "Sitting in my car with tears running down my face."

A half second later, my phone rang. I shifted in my seat and took a deep breath. Here we go. "Hello," I mumbled into the phone.

"What's wrong?" Sarah shrieked with panic in her voice.

"I'm fine. I just got rocked by the final episode of this podcast called *Dying for Sex*." I hesitated to tell her. I was sure it sounded odd, dying for sex. She and I had never had sex.

I had been listening to the final episode of the podcast series called *Dying for Sex*.[13] I generally don't listen to pod-

---

13   Nikki Boyer, "Becoming Whole," March 11, 2020 in Dying for Sex, produced by Wondery, podcast, MP3 audio, 18:46.

casts with sex in the title, but this one caught my eye. I like sex and hate dying so I thought it might be interesting.

The podcast was a narrative between two best friends from California: Nikki, the podcast host, and Molly, her best friend who was dying of stage-four breast cancer. Over the course of six episodes, they talked about Molly's wild escapades—sex with guys she met on dating apps—she decided to have before she died.

Molly was a forty-five-year-old woman who had recently divorced her husband of ten years. She decided, since she was dying, to have some fun and feel alive while she still had time. With the help of dating apps and her amazing personality, she met several guys over the course of a year as she battled hospital visits and her deteriorating condition.

The two girls giggled as Molly recounted some of the more bizarre dating encounters she had experienced. On one occasion, a guy got naked in her hospital room. Another guy orgasmed out of his backseat car door in the middle of an upper-class neighborhood as they made out like a couple of high school kids. The stories were hilarious.

I caught myself laughing out loud and falling in love with Molly. She was full of energy and wildly open about her life and adventure. She was humble, kind, unpretentious, and inviting.

Over the course of the first five episodes, Molly never cried. She was always in good spirits, even when she could barely breathe. She joked about the crazy dates and complicated sexual experiences. Complicated because the cancer riddled her body and she knew there couldn't be a future with any of the men. Complicated because some dudes were into some wild things.

In the last episode, Nikki asked Molly what she thought about dying. Through tears and breathless pauses, she said the adventure had taught her how to be whole again. She learned to forgive the man who molested her when she was eight, forgive her mother, forgive her ex-husband, and forgive herself. She found peace in becoming whole again.

"This disease took away my ability to book travel, buy tickets to shows, and set dates with people. I realized the other day that there is a trip planned just for me, and I don't know where it is or when it is or what it is going to be like, but it's all mine. I am really looking forward to it because it is going to be the first real trip I've taken in a truly long time because it is one that's not going to make me sick or not make me in more pain. And it will be easy, loving, colorful, and adventurous," she said in a quiet, shaky voice, pausing to catch her breath every few moments.

My heart was breaking as I sat in the front seat of my car, hiding in a Starbucks parking lot and avoiding eye contact with humans walking by.

Then, as if I wasn't already an emotional basket case, Molly said one last thing. "The person I get the gift of falling in love with when I die is myself."

And the tears busted down my face as I slumped in my seat. An ugly cry. The kind where my face contorts, and I look like a moose.

In the end, Molly found love for herself. She died on March 8, 2019.

Self-love. That oddly powerful, confusing, and complicated force that makes us or breaks us. Those of us who don't have it, desperately want it. Those of us who do have it, don't understand how someone couldn't have it.

I believe self-love is a fancy term for self-acceptance. Until we can accept ourselves, we cannot love ourselves. Accepting ourselves is the key.

Dr. Zach Bush was being interviewed by Rich Roll on a podcast recently. He works in ICU with hospice.

At the end of the podcast, Dr. Bush went on a monologue about what he has observed working with end-of-life patients.

He shared his experience with people he has saved after they technically died. He said they all say the same thing when they wake back up.

"There is one sentence that came back again and again," he told Rich with a look of deep concentration on his face. "I had one ICU shift that was very weird…I worked for thirty-six hours, and during that night, my shift, I see three people die, and I bring them all back." He looked up with big eyes. "And to the last one of those three, their first sentence was, 'why did you bring me back?'" A hopeful smile formed on his face.[14]

He continued. "Then as they start to get oriented and in the hours that follow, they are telling their loved ones, 'I went into this space and there was bright, white light everywhere and in that moment, I felt completely accepted for the first time in my life.'" He paused. "That was an unexpected sentence to hear from multiple accounts. I felt completely accepted for the first time in my life."[15]

Dr. Zack Bush and Molly would probably agree with me, though. I don't think we need to face death to find love and acceptance for ourselves. I think it is right here, right now. We are enough. Always have been, always will be. And as soon as we believe it, we find love.

---

14   Rich Roll, "The Best Monologue EVER: Zach Bush, MD | Rich Roll Podcast," Jan 9, 2019, video, 4:28.

15   Ibid.

LOVE LESSONS

1. Practice acceptance. Don't wait until you are dying to start fully accepting yourself. Talk to friends about acceptance, google acceptance, and get obsessed with acceptance.

2. Be a best friend when it's the hardest to be one. We all need each other, especially near the end. Be there for your loved ones, your family, and your friends when they are coming to the end of life. Step up and show up.

3. Have a one-night stand at least once in your life.

25

TWO BEST FRIENDS

————

"Love is like a banana. If you leave it alone for too long, it's no good anymore."

— ZACHARY, FOURTEEN YEARS OLD

"What the hell?!" Anthony shouted at his friend in the front seat.[16]

In a whisper of panic, Anthony said, "There is a white lady back there." He pointed to the back seat of the car.[17]

Lester had to pull over. He was laughing too hard to drive.

"That is the GPS," Lester laughed. Anthony thought there was a white lady in the car when it was the GPS saying *one tenth of a mile turn right*.[18] Anthony had not been in a car in thirty years.

————

16 "EP. #103: Anthony Ray Hinton, Part 2: Finding Life, Hope and Redemption on Death Row," January 6, 2019, in Super Soul Podcast, produced by Harpo Studios Super Soul Sunday, LLC, YouTube Video, 30:20.

17 "EP. #103: Anthony Ray Hinton, Part 2: Finding Life, Hope and Redemption on Death Row," January 6, 2019, in *Super Soul Podcast, produced by Harpo Studios Super Soul Sunday, LLC,* YouTube Video, 29:20.

18 "EP. #103: Anthony Ray Hinton, Part 2: Finding Life, Hope and Redemption on Death Row," January 6, 2019, in Super Soul Podcast, produced by Harpo Studios Super Soul Sunday, LLC, YouTube Video, 30:25.

I couldn't help but laugh along as I listened to the banter between Anthony and Lester, best friends since they were four and six respectively, on the *Super Soul Podcast* as they drove away from prison. I imagined the scene of them pulling away from the prison where Anthony was caged for thirty years.

When I first heard the story of Anthony and Lester, it floored me. Ripped my heart out and squeezed it to death. Not so much because Anthony was wrongfully locked up in a tiny cell for thirty years, but because of his two interesting friends; Lester and Henry. Talk about a lesson in compassion, empathy, and love. Grab some tissues.

Anthony Ray Hinton was twenty-nine years old when two police arrested him in the front yard of his house. He was cutting the grass. His mother was inside. It was 1985, and he was charged with murder, a crime he never committed. A poor black man in a white courtroom.

He remained on death row in Alabama for twenty-eight years, where his legs were longer than his metal bed. Fifty-four men and one woman were escorted past his cell to their executions over the course of his three decades in prison.

"The hardest part was the smell," Anthony told Oprah Winfrey, talking about living thirty feet away from the execution room. "Of all the fifty-four, I asked a guard officer, 'Is there anything you can give me so I won't have to smell their flesh burning?' That officer looked at me and said, 'No, there is nothing that I can give you. You'll get used to it, and one day somebody will smell your flesh burning.'"[19]

Anthony's story is remarkable. In 1985, a spree of restaurant robberies left two managers dead and one shot but not

19 "EP.#102: Anthony Ray Hinton, Part 1: Freedom After 30 Years on Death Row," January 5, 2019, in Super Soul Podcast, produced by Harpo Studios Super Soul Sunday, LLC, YouTube Video, 20:20.

critically wounded. The manager who survived picked Anthony out of a photo lineup, even though Anthony was at work in a warehouse at the time of the robbery. The police, looking for a quick fix, found an old gun Anthony's mother owned and tied it to the robberies and murders.[20]

"The prosecutor—who had a documented history of racial bias and said he could tell Mr. Hinton was guilty and "evil" solely from his appearance—told the court that the State's experts' asserted match between Mrs. Hinton's gun and the bullets from all three crimes was the only evidence linking Mr. Hinton to the Davidson and Vason murders."[21]

That is called the shit end of a stick. The Alabama criminal justice system failed Anthony, and since he had no money to buy fancy lawyers, the prosecution won. He didn't speak during his first three years in prison. Not one word. Silent, angry, and innocent.

Thirty years later, at fifty-nine years of age, Anthony was exonerated and released from prison. Equal Justice Initiative attorneys took on his case and fought for over twelve years to free him. "The judge finally dismissed the charges after prosecutors said that scientists at the Alabama Department of Forensic Sciences tested the evidence and confirmed that the crime bullets cannot be matched to the Hinton weapon."[22]

Anthony had a best friend who he met on death row, an inmate named Henry. One night, after Anthony had been in prison for three years, he heard Henry crying in the cell next to him. In an act of compassion, Anthony called to him through the wall and asked what was wrong. Henry said his mother had died.

---

20 "Anthony Ray Hinton," Equal Justice Initiative, accessed September 19, 2020.

21 Ibid.

22 Ibid.

"At an early age, my mom taught me compassion," he explained to Oprah, she said "no matter what one does in life, they still deserve compassion. And it was that compassion that I hollered through the brick wall...I said, 'Hey, is there something wrong?' It took him a while to respond, but he finally said, 'I got word my mother passed.' And I told him that I was sorry and told him a corny joke, and we kinda laughed just a little bit. I laid back down, and the next morning I had my voice and humor back," Anthony recalled about speaking to Henry and breaking his own three-year silence.[23]

The two men lived next to each other in joining cells. Though they never saw each other, they became best friends. Henry was executed by the electric chair in 1997. Throughout the course of their friendship, Anthony learned that Henry's father was the Grand Wizard of the Ku Klux Klan. Henry was a leader as well, and he was on death row because he cut the genitals off of a nineteen-year-old black boy and hung him.

I was struck by the insanity of a black man wrongfully accused by a white justice system and a white supremacist who murdered a black boy becoming best friends on death row.

Anthony explained to Oprah why he had compassion for Henry. "What I knew is when you are hanging at the end of a rope, does it matter what color the hand is that reaches up to help you? What I knew was he loved his mother like I loved my mother, and I could understand his pain."[24]

---

23   "EP.#102: Anthony Ray Hinton, Part 1: Freedom After 30 Years on Death Row," January 5, 2019, in Super Soul Podcast, produced by Harpo Studios Super Soul Sunday, LLC, YouTube Video, 30:21.

24   "EP.#102: Anthony Ray Hinton, Part 1: Freedom After 30 Years on Death Row," January 5, 2019, in Super Soul Podcast, produced by Harpo Studios Super Soul Sunday, LLC, YouTube Video, 30:09.

Both of Anthony's friendships were profound to me. A true lesson in compassion. He helped Henry, a former KKK member, forgive his father and himself so he could die with love in his heart. Then there was Lester, his best friend from childhood. Lester had a labor job working a night shift from 11:00 p.m. to 7:00 a.m. every day in their hometown of Birmingham, Alabama. However, he drove to visit Anthony in prison every Saturday. Not just any Saturday, but every Saturday for thirty YEARS!

"At 9:15, he was there. Like clockwork," Anthony told Oprah. Lester would get off work at 7:00 a.m. and drive 268 miles, one way, to the prison to see his friend Anthony. Every. Single. Saturday.[25]

I found a video of the two men sitting beside each other at Oprah's house in Hawaii. Both men were in their sixties and a little thick around the corners. They had Southern accents and a simple way about them. A kindness you often find in country folks.

As I watched the interview on Oprah's porch with the beautiful ocean behind them, I wondered about Lester. What made him drive 836,160 miles, or around nine thousand hours, without sleep to be there for his friend? I thought about how bittersweet it was he was now thousands of miles away from home at Oprah Winfrey's house in Hawaii. An experience of a lifetime, sitting next to his best friend, because he never gave up on Anthony.

Friendship might be the most important love of all.

Anthony's mother taught him compassion. Henry taught him forgiveness. Lester taught him friendship. They all taught me love. A beautiful tragedy.

---

25   "Oprah Winfrey Facebook Live with Anthony Ray Hinton," June 28, 2018, Youtube Video, 31:21.

LOVE LESSONS

1. I believe human beings are born with compassion for each other. It is what draws us together. Compassion is a critical element of love. It sees no color. It believes in one another. It is the pain we feel in our hearts for another person.

2. How do I show up for my friends? Like clockwork? Or do I need to do some work? Showing up builds trust, connection, and love. Let's keep showing up for each other.

3. Enjoy the rain. Life is hard sometimes, but we can still enjoy the rain. Anthony was telling Oprah about his niece who recently tried to hand him an umbrella as he was getting out of the car in the rain. "No," he told her, "I'm gonna walk in the rain. For thirty years, not a drop of rain was allowed on my body. So let me enjoy this rain."[26]

---

26 "EP.#102: Anthony Ray Hinton, Part 1: Freedom After 30 Years on Death Row," January 5, 2019, in Super Soul Podcast, produced by Harpo Studios Super Soul Sunday, LLC, YouTube Video, 28:15.

26

KEVIN'S CRAZY LOVE

"Love is bananas because they are yummy"

– LAINEY, THREE AND A HALF YEARS OLD

Kevin clawed his way back to the surface of the water. He could sense a massive animal swimming beneath him. Hoping it would not kill him, he started punching at the shadow. This was odd, because he had just jumped off the Golden Gate Bridge in an attempt to take his own life. And was still alive. Barely.

I sat across from Kevin in the basement of his home recently. We both drank coffee out of superhero mugs. Mine was Captain America, his was Batman. Kevin sat straight up, with beaming eyes, a shaved head, and lots of freckles. He stared attentively at me. He had put on weight since I saw him last. Not too much, but noticeable. Usually he is strapped with muscles. Now he was a little soft around the waist and a bit fuller in the face. Later he explained his new medicine prevented him from feeling full when eating meals. So he would just keep eating. Sounded awful.

In 2000, Kevin Hines jumped off the Golden Gate Bridge. He traveled 240 feet in four seconds and shattered his back and ankle on impact. The force of the fall pushed him seventy feet below the surface of the water where, in a panic, he realized he did not want to die. Somehow, he made his way back up to the surface. However, he was having trouble staying afloat. That's when the shark appeared under him.

Or did it?

Over 1,600 suicide attempts have been recorded at the Golden Gate Bridge. Only thirty-six people have survived the fall. Kevin is one of only five who can walk.

A few years after his jump, he was a guest on a local talk show telling his remarkable story. He mentioned the terror he felt as the shark circled under him after he decided he wanted to live. A man was watching the show and called in to say he was happy to hear Kevin survived. The man was on the bridge that day and saw Kevin jump. He told Kevin the creature wasn't a shark, but a sea lion. After Kevin blacked out from his massive injuries, the sea lion kept him afloat for seven minutes until the coast guard arrived. Without the sea lion, there would be no Kevin Hines.

I didn't go over to Kevin's house to talk about suicide, the jump, or sea lions. Rather, I wanted to hear his love story. The craziest love story of all time. A story about an insane man falling in love with a sane woman in an insane asylum.

Kevin has been in nine psychiatric wards since his jump. On his eighth stay, he was issued twenty-six electroconvulsive therapy (ECT) treatments. He said the doctors put him under with anesthesia and forced a massive electric shock to his brain. It turned off and restarted his brain.

"I had been suicidal for sixty straight days. It was the last resort. It worked!" he said in his animated style. He talked quickly and feverishly. Like a kid trying to explain a cool new toy.

Kevin currently lives in Atlanta with his wife of thirteen years. He travels the world to speak about suicide prevention and was one of the stars of the documentary *The Bridge.*

"What is love?" I started the conversation. He sat with perfect posture and his hands on the arm rests of the chair. The room was bare except for two chairs, a coffee table between them, and a camera tripod he uses to create videos for his YouTube channel.

He looked up and thought for a moment, then said, "An effervescent light. It's always hopeful. It's always endearing. And if you do it right, it's always true."

Good answer, I thought. There I was, sitting across from a man who had battled mental illness his whole life and somehow found an amazing woman who he has since been married to for thirteen years. A man who had jumped off the damn Golden Gate Bridge. I freak out on six-foot ladders.

"How did you meet Margaret?" I sipped my coffee.

"I knew she would be the rest of my life the moment I looked in her eyes." A big smile formed across his face. There was no hesitation in his answer. Love at first sight.

He started telling me his love story.

Kevin had been in the psychiatric ward for months and was feeling better. He conned the staff into letting him help to kill the boredom. One day, while he was wearing khaki pants and a button-up shirt he'd stolen from the lost and found, holding a stolen clipboard and acting like a volunteer, he got a tap on the shoulder.

He turned around and saw Margaret for the first time. She was in the lobby, as was he, looking to visit her cousin who was a patient. He fell in love. Instantly.

"I remember her eyes were almond brown, sexy, cool, and I was done," he said poetically.

"Excuse me," she said. "Do you work here?"

"Sure," he quickly replied as he nervously looked over at the staff behind the check-in counter, hoping they would not call his bluff. They smiled, and he mouthed "thank you" silently. He turned and escorted her to see her cousin who was a patient as well.

"Your orderly is very nice," she said to her cousin, pointing to Kevin as they arrived at his room.

"What? Kevin? He is crazy! He jumps off bridges! Stay away from him!" her cousin yelled.

Her cousin was a young guy who entered the ward in a catatonic state. He had overdosed on drugs and was not moving or speaking. Kevin made it his mission to get him to talk. He felt sorry for him because nobody was giving him any attention. Kevin would sit and tell him stories day after day. Two weeks later, the cousin finally screamed out, "Jesus Christ, man, you talk too much! Leave me alone!"

"I celebrated because I finally got him to talk!" Kevin acted out the scene for me.

Margaret continued to visit her cousin every few days, and on one occasion Kevin asked her if he could buy her coffee. She said, "Oh honey, hell no."

We both laughed. Kevin had a lightheartedness to him.

Margaret was raised in a large family in the San Francisco area. She joined Wall Street out of college and became very successful in business. Not the kind of woman who you assume dates insane men.

Eventually Kevin was released from the hospital into a halfway home. After thirty days, he was granted his first chance to leave due to good behavior. He jumped at the opportunity and called Margaret to see if she would go on a date with him.

"How did you get her number?" I asked, wondering why a sane woman would give an insane man her number.

"Her cousin's file," he said with a smirk. We both laughed. Smooth move, my friend.

"Who's this?" Margaret asked as she answered the phone.

"This is Kevin, from the hospital."

"Oh no, no," she shrieked.

He asked her on a date, and she said no. Again. Obviously.

"Okay, Margaret, listen, I need this. I just need one date, and if it goes South, you never have to see me again," he pleaded.

"Fine Kevin, one date," Margaret reluctantly replied.

Damn, I thought. Kevin has some serious confidence. I'm terrified of asking girls out and don't live in a mental institution. Maybe I should.

He showed up at her apartment at 8:00 p.m. on a Friday night. They had a reservation at a mafia-run Italian joint at 9:00 p.m. Kevin stood in her doorway with a huge duffle bag. She asked why he had the duffle bag, and he informed her the halfway home locked the doors at 9:00 p.m. on Friday nights and didn't open until Monday morning.

"OH, HELL NO!" Kevin mimicked Margaret adamantly refusing to let him stay with her. We both laughed. Again, I was thinking, damn this guy is persistent. He promised he would sleep on a bench in the rain if she would just go to dinner with him.

"Well, it gets worse." Kevin smiled at me.

"You made the reservation at a restaurant?" I wondered how he figured that out on his own.

"No, she made the reservations," he replied. Brave girl, I thought.

The restaurant table was tiny. The joint was small and crowded. Kevin was wearing his only white shirt which he bought for five dollars at Old Navy.

"It was Caffe Sport, in San Francisco. Now at Caffe Sport, you don't order, they order for you," he continued, and in rhythm said, "They look at you, they judge you, and they order for you!"

"Oh, so they order for you?" An image of a small, mafia, fancy Italian place entered my mind. My immediate thought was the old *Saturday Night Live* skits where they had a couple of tables and an annoying waiter.

"Yes, and I have a lot of allergies. This was not a good situation." He pointed his finger in the air.

They brought Margaret a nice chicken parmesan and Kevin a lobster tail, spaghetti, boiling hot butter, and a weird lemon wedge. He swears they did it to ruin his night and possibly his life.

"I am freaking out because I have never had a lobster in my life. Never even cracked a lobster in my life." He looked at me with panic in his face.

Personally, I can't imagine anything worse on a first date than lobster. Well, actually, spaghetti might be the worst. Eating on a first date is awkward as is, but you add in a dish that takes an acrobat to manage, and the result is usually a disaster. Moving food into your mouth while trying to have a surface-level conversation with a girl you like is a dangerous process. Maybe I am just an idiot.

"I said a prayer and then cracked the tail. Marinara sauce went all over my white shirt. I thought this was getting ridiculous. I said to myself, 'Kevin, calm down, do something classy.' So I picked up the lemon wedge. I looked at it. I looked at the lobster tail. I looked at Margaret. I started shaking a little, and I went like this…" Kevin made a motion with his right hand punching straight out in front of him. He squeezed the damn lemon, and it shot directly into her right eye.

I've had some bad dates, but lord help me…this was a disaster.

The lady at the table next to them asked if Margaret was okay. The whole place was watching the spectacle at this point. Kevin said his inner dialogue started telling him to do something classy fast to save the situation.

"So I grab the butter and some of it spilled and shot straight across the table onto her chest. Then I panicked and tried to wipe it off with my napkin. RIGHT ON HER BREASTS! Then I hear the two words a guy never wants to hear on a date." He paused.

"What two words?" I anxiously asked.

"CHECK PLEASE!" He shot his finger in the air.

The walk back to Margaret's apartment was silent and awkward. Kevin knew he'd blown it. She was one hundred paces ahead of him the entire way. Once they arrived at her place, they stared at each other awkwardly.

"Let's go to the roof," Margaret finally said, feeling compassion for Kevin but still unwilling to let him into her apartment.

"Are you going to throw me off?" Kevin kind of joked, but also wasn't sure.

"No, Kevin, let's go," she sighed.

They made it to the roof, laid down on two yoga mats, and stared at the moon. It was a clear night. Margaret remained silent. Kevin couldn't take the silence and asked, "Margaret, what are we doing up here?" He was starting to panic. He already ruined her eye, burned her chest, and made a fool out of both of them at her favorite restaurant.

"Kevin, if all we do is stare at that full moon, then nothing else can possibly go wrong tonight," she replied as she stared at the moon.

Kevin relaxed and told her his entire story. His troubled childhood, mental illness, and everything in-between.

"When I opened up to her and told my story, she saw the real me," Kevin told me.

They eventually started dating, and the rest is history. Margaret has learned to live with Kevin's mental illness, and Kevin has found something and someone to live for besides himself. He has turned his story into a motivational force for thousands of people around the world. He also is madly in love with his wife.

Their story is powerful. A story about commitment, persistence, perseverance, and overcoming challenges. A story about love actually winning.

We finished up our conversation and headed upstairs to where Margaret was working in the kitchen.

"How did it go?" she asked us, smiling up from the sink. There was a way she and Kevin looked at each other. I could only describe it as love. True love for each other.

I joked with both of them about the crazy love story. How he kept asking her on dates even though she shut him down each time

I turned to Kevin and asked, "Why did you keep asking her out after so many rejections?"

"Persistence is the key to love, mental health, and psych wards!" he said with a huge laugh.

LOVE LESSONS

1. When looking for love, persistence is critical. We cannot give up that easily. We have to keep dating, keep trying, keep putting ourselves out there. We have to quickly get over rejection. Finding the right person for you is a numbers game. Kevin was fearless and kept on trying when courting Margaret.

2. A key to a successful, long-term relationship is commitment. Margaret could have left Kevin a million times but committed to the relationship thirteen years ago. When she told her mother she was going to marry Kevin, her mother warned her about how hard her life was going to be living with a person with mental illness. Margaret accepted and committed to Kevin. Their love has grown deep even though there have been some very hard times along the way.

3. Kevin's motto is #beheretomorrow. He fights to spread the message that we all matter and suicide is never the answer. I asked him if he still has suicidal thoughts. He said he does frequently. I asked how he deals with the thoughts. "When I have a suicidal thought, I have a rule that I have to turn to the closest person near me and tell them I am having suicidal thoughts, regardless if I know them or not." If you are struggling, reach out to someone and tell them. We are all the same, we all suffer. Do not think you are the only one. The National Suicide Prevention Hotline is 1-800-273-8255.

27

BOB'S LOVE LETTER

———

"Only once in your life, I truly believe, you find someone who can completely turn your world around. You tell them things that you've never shared with another soul and they absorb everything you say and actually want to hear more. You share hopes for the future, dreams that will never come true, goals that were never achieved and the many disappointments life has thrown at you. When something wonderful happens, you can't wait to tell them about it, knowing they will share in your excitement. They are not embarrassed to cry with you when you are hurting or laugh with you when you make a fool of yourself. Never do they hurt your feelings or make you feel like you are not good enough, but rather they build you up and show you the things about yourself that make you special and even beautiful. There is never any pressure, jealousy or competition but only a quiet calmness when they are around. You can be yourself and not worry about what they will think of you because they love you for who you are. The things that seem insignificant to most people such as a note, song or walk become invaluable treasures kept safe in your heart to cherish forever. Memories of your childhood come back and are so clear and vivid it's like being young

again. Colors seem brighter and more brilliant. Laughter seems part of daily life where before it was infrequent or didn't exist at all. A phone call or two during the day helps to get you through a long day's work and always brings a smile to your face. In their presence, there's no need for continuous conversation, but you find you're quite content in just having them nearby. Things that never interested you before become fascinating because you know they are important to this person who is so special to you. You think of this person on every occasion and in everything you do. Simple things bring them to mind like a pale blue sky, gentle wind or even a storm cloud on the horizon. You open your heart knowing that there's a chance it may be broken one day and in opening your heart, you experience a love and joy that you never dreamed possible. You find that being vulnerable is the only way to allow your heart to feel true pleasure that's so real it scares you. You find strength in knowing you have a true friend and possibly a soul mate who will remain loyal to the end. Life seems completely different, exciting and worthwhile. Your only hope and security is in knowing that they are a part of your life."[27]

BOB MARLEY

LOVE LESSONS

1. Life is better shared.

2. Love is the essence of hope.

---

27 J. Dorlita, "Bob Marley Quote on Love," Private Love Letters (blog), January 23, 2013.

3. Recklessly fall in love, sing wildly in the shower, dance under the moon. Kiss with the passion of a thousand stars and turn your face to the warm sun. Breathe in sunsets, laugh till sunrise, and kiss every inch of your lover.

28

LOVE IS MAGIC

———

"Bananas are like love because they get squishy if you push too hard."

DYLAN, SEVEN YEARS OLD

I sat in the car, staring at the house. It was a brick house atop a small hill covered in grass. A lady stood peering out of the glass front door. My friend Ilene was in the passenger seat of my car.

I took a breath, finished my Starbucks iced latte, and headed up the hill to meet her. She had white hair, combat boots, and a normal nose. I entered the house and followed her into the basement. She sat on the couch. I sat on the other end. Ilene sat in a chair that was awkwardly tiny. I thought this woman might have some insight on my search to understand love. Or at a minimum, one hell of a story.

"I consider myself a witch," she announced. She was wearing a black shirt-dress. Is that what you call it? Not sure.

Ilene found the witch online and asked if I could interview her. Ilene isn't scared of witches. That makes one of us.

The witch seemed nervous. Her arms were crossed, hugging her chest as she peered at me. Her feet dangled a few inches from the floor. Motionless. A few tattoos were scattered on her arms in various shapes and designs. If I had to guess her age, I would say she was fifty years old, but I am not good at guessing witch ages.

The witch, who went by Dia, was a polyamorous, ethical non-monogamist high priestess of a pagan coven. Read that sentence again if you want to fry your brain. She had been married for nineteen years to her second husband, loved dogs, and was a psychic medium. Okay, let's all take a breath.

Tony, her husband, was not a witch. He was an engineer and stayed upstairs sewing a leather belt on a vintage sewing machine. Her dogs roamed the house.

"What is your definition of love?" I fiddled with my small notebook and pen, kicking off the interview.

She thought for a moment, then replied, "Love is the unconditional acceptance of another being."

Not bad, I thought. I have asked a ton of people that question, and nobody has ever had the same answer. However, many use the word "unconditional."

"For example, I love my dogs unconditionally even though they vomited all over my carpet this morning." She smiled. Maybe they were witch dogs.

She continued, "I think unconditional love requires the 'big three.'"

1. Do not keep score.

2. Have respect for the other person.

3. Don't raise your voice.

Those were her rules. I asked the witch how many times she had been in love. She told me "a lot," which I thought was a great answer. Most people say two or three times. Free spirits and hippies say a lot. I think a great life would be one where you fall in love a lot.

Curious about the man upstairs, I asked, "How did you meet your husband?"

"I cast a spell," she replied matter-of-factly.

"Really?" I perked up, hoping this might be the answer to mankind's quest for love. Magic.

"So what happened was I kept dating the wrong men," she sighed. "I decided my picker was off, and I was attracted to the wrong types of men. So I wrote down on a piece of paper all the things I thought I wanted in a man. And then I burned it. I took out another piece of paper and wrote down what I did not want in a man. He can't be an axe murderer. Can't be a pedophile or rapist. Can't be a drug addict. Can't be an alcoholic and has to be gainfully employed. And that was about it. I mean, I really left it open."

We both laughed at the list of deal-breakers. Pretty straightforward, I thought. No losers, murderers, or crack-heads. Nobody wants to end up on a Netflix special or *Dateline*.

She carried on smiling at me. "I petitioned the gods and said the deal is I'm going to date myself, and no one else. I'm just going to date myself until I meet the person who I think I would **never** date. And then I will go out with that person because all the men I was attracted to before were the wrong kind of men."

"So you basically forced yourself to date guys you were not interested in because your date picker was broken?" My head was spinning.

"Exactly!" She held up her finger. "So I got set up by a Methodist minister, not lying!" Her voice raised an octave.

"The Methodist minister owned a recording studio. I was singing backup for pagan chant CDs in the same recording studio. Tony was a recording engineer. Okay, so the owner of the studio met me and said I know this guy who's single you should meet. I said no, I'm not dating anybody."

The minister secretly invited both of them to the studio one day. They all showed up. A pagan witch, her son, a Methodist minister, and a Christian engineer. A motley crew to say the least.

"So now here we are, and I am mortified because the first thing this man does is say, 'Hi I'm Tony. I'm a Christian,' and I'm a known pagan, right?" She looked at both of us. "And I'm like, okay, great. And he has on a shirt that says 'grab her booty and pinch' with two people doing it on the shirt. As I looked at him, I could hear angelic laughter in my head. I was like, I gotta date this guy. Oh my god!"

She slapped her knee. "Sure enough, at the end of the night, he asked my son Sam if he wanted to go to a carousel in Chattanooga. Sam said, 'I have to take my mom,' and he goes, 'well okay we can let her come.' And so that was our first date. We sat under the bridge and talked and talked. At the end of it, I was like 'I'm totally marrying this guy.' I left knowing I was gonna marry him."

Fifteen years into the marriage, she and Tony decided to try polygamy.

"We needed to figure out a way to inject some new energy into our relationship." She explained about the decision to try polygamy. She told me polygamy was not foreign to her because many people in the pagan community practice it.

"What is the secret to making polygamy work?" I asked curiously. The idea of a husband having a girlfriend who is friends with the husband's wife who also has a boyfriend makes my head explode. Too much math.

"A poly therapist," she quickly replied.

She explained she and Tony hired a poly therapist before deciding to become polyamorous. "This is critical," she assured me. "It is also essential to create rules and boundaries."

"How do you deal with jealousy?" I thought back to a podcast I heard where a scientist claimed the reason polygamy doesn't make sense for humans is because of jealousy.

"I haven't felt jealous yet." She looked up, thinking. "I am not sure about him. For us, we have specific rules which help, I think. For example, we are only allowed to go on dates if each of us has a date at the same time."

"Huh?" I looked over at Ilene.

"Tony was supposed to be visiting his girlfriend this weekend, and my boyfriend was going to come to stay with me. However, Tony's plans got canceled, so I had to cancel mine as part of the rule," she explained.

Rules. I suppose rules are critical for any relationship. Or agreements. Many relationships fail because the partners don't set up rules or agreements prior to making a commitment to each other.

I asked her about her childhood. It didn't sound pleasant.

She was raised in an abusive household with two other siblings. "We dealt with incest, rape, and abuse. The only beacon of light was my grandmother, who was a devout Southern Baptist living in Southern Georgia. She was also a seer."

A seer, as the witch explained, is a psychic. Ah yes, folks who can talk to dead people and whatnot, I thought. The world of woo-woo and prophecy. Crystal balls and weird tarot cards with wizards and wolves on them. Got it.

She sat back and closed her eyes. "People would bring my grandmother gifts to prophesize for them. They would bring her a chicken and ask if their husbands were cheating on them."

"Would she tell them?" I asked.

"Yes," she said with a sly smile.

Be careful, gentlemen. You never know when your old lady might gift a chicken to a psychic to find out if you are sexting your secretary. If you only learn one thing from this book...

"Can you see dead people?" I cautiously asked.

"Yes."

I looked around the room.

A half hour into our conversation, she relaxed a bit. Her shoulders dropped and her face softened. I got her to laugh. She got me to laugh. She was an actual human being.

"Do you love yourself?" I finally asked toward the end of our conversation.

"Yes." She nodded confidently.

"Have you always loved yourself?" I wondered aloud.

"No," she replied. "I only started loving myself around five years ago. It was a long, hard road from eighteen years of abuse and all the negative programming during my childhood to loving myself now."

She openly told me therapy saved her. Years of cognitive behavioral therapy helped her overcome all of the trauma of her past.

My last therapist explained cognitive behavioral therapy as talk therapy, where you meet with a therapist regularly and talk through challenges. He was a weirdo.

"Are there any rituals or spells to help somebody love themselves?" I asked, hoping she would say it was a witch's brew of spider legs and Jolly Ranchers.

"I think the best thing you can do is stand in front of a mirror three times a day and tell yourself that you are lovable. It sounds crazy simple, but it is wholly effective because it is hard. Think about how hard it is sometimes to just look strangers in the eye. Then compare that to forcing yourself to look into your own eyes and plant that seed of love on a regular and consistent basis. It will change how you look at yourself," she affirmed.

She was right. How simple and how hard at the same time. I went to a therapist who told me to look in a mirror and say "I love you" every day. It took me two weeks to have the courage to just stand in front of the damn mirror. Then it took me a couple days to look into my own eyes. Finally, I said "I love you" while looking into my own eyes, and the floodgates opened. I bawled. What a mess. It grew easier, though, and now I can do it and actually believe what I am saying. Magic, I guess.

An hour into the conversation, my ADHD was skyrocketing, and I had to pee. I decided to ask a final question. "Why do you think love is so hard for people?"

Her eyebrows creased and she touched her chin. "I think it can be hard for people, first, because they don't love themselves, and second, because they didn't have role models for love."

I couldn't agree more. My father never expressed his emotions around me, and he always called my mother horrible names. I had no brothers or sisters, and my mom worked all hours to support us. I learned about love from MTV and *Cosmopolitan* magazines I stole out of trash cans.

I found Dia to be one of the wisest people I have talked to about love. Her answers were thoughtful, simple, and elegant. She was soft, humble, and authentic. She openly talked about her abusive past, current struggles, and thoughts on love.

Dia is a high priestess who leads a coven of followers. She is a human being, wife, mother, and dog owner. She has degrees in journalism, psychology, and theatre. She was well-spoken and extremely intelligent.

"What does your son think about your lifestyle?" I asked, wondering what her twenty-one-year-old son thought of her polyamorous lifestyle.

"He thinks we are crazy," she laughed.

There is no rule book on love. There is no rule book on how to love. Each of our journeys are different, but I think we are all after the same things: love, growth, connection, and spirituality.

LOVE LESSONS

1. The path to self-love includes therapy, mirror work, and reprogramming your brain. It takes asking for help and doing the work. Shifting from a belief of worthlessness to worthiness. We are all worthy, but we don't all believe so. Dia taught me it is a long journey toward reversing the traumas of our past, but there is a light at the end of the tunnel.

2. The path to finding a new partner is to audit and look for historical patterns in your past relationships. Do you date the same type of men or women every time? Do you end up in healthy relationships or unhealthy relationships? Make a change even though it does not feel natural yet. Choose the opposite and see what happens. Figure out exactly what you want and exactly what you don't want and offer it to the universe in the form of prayer, ritual, or black magic!

3. Hire a poly therapist if you are thinking about having a polyamorous relationship.

29

THIRTY-SIX THINGS

—

"Bananas are like love because they are yellow just like sunshine."
THOMAS, SEVEN YEARS OLD

Bill lived in a cult. Not just any cult, but a fun, sex-fueled, contro-versial cult formed by the Indian sex guru Bhagwan Shree Rajneesh, also known as Osho. I watched the remarkable documentary about this robe-wearing, white-haired guru who literally built his own city in America. In an article titled, "The Free-Love Cult that Terrorized America—and became Netflix's Latest Must-Watch," *The Guardian* reported the following about Osho and his followers:

"By the 1980s he was at odds with the government in India and so decided to buy a ranch in Oregon. The land was largely uninhabitable, but he sent his followers ahead to create a utopian paradise. They built a giant dam, an airport, an electricity station, and a meditation centre that could hold ten thousand people. They called it Rajneeshpuram, and when it was ready, Rajneesh and his followers relocated to the US."[28]

---

28 Sam Wolfson, "The Free-Love Cult that Terrorized America—and Became Netflix's Latest Must-Watch," *The Guardian*, April 7, 2018, U.S Edition.

Sounds like a good time to me. I like good times, weirdos, and controversy. All of his followers wore a mix of red and maroon clothing like an army of red ants. A bona fide bunch of freaks.

I met a gal one day who mentioned she and her father spent a summer at Rajneeshpuram. She was sixteen when they joined the community.

"It was so fun! We danced all the time!" she said about her experience in the cult. I insisted she introduce me to her father so I could ask him a million questions about love. She set up a meeting at his apartment. Finally, I would have a cult member friend. Fingers crossed.

The apartment was modest, in a dated building just outside of Atlanta, which was a long way from Bill's roots in New York. I arrived around noon and knocked on his door. I was expecting him to appear in a monk's robe with a magical staff and a dreamcatcher necklace. He opened the door wearing jeans and a white t-shirt. Boring.

He was taller than I expected. An athletic-looking dude in his seventies. The apartment looked basic with bland, tan carpet, a nondescript couch, and a boring round, wooden kitchen table. So far, he scored a zero on my mystical guru cult member stereotyping. We settled down at his kitchen table and began the interview. He was boldly confident as he told the story of his life. His posture was perfect. I always notice people's posture. Mainly because mine sucks, and my friend Jolly, who lives in the bus, told me the key to self-esteem is perfect posture. Now it haunts me. His back was straight, head high, shoulders back. I was jealous.

During Bill's seventy-four years on this planet, he has accomplished some outrageous things. He was born on an Air Force base during World War II and had always had a deep urge to fly airplanes. Over the course of his life, he has flown fourteen different aircrafts.

"I used to always dream that I was drowning. I'm sure it is because I was born on an Air Force base during World War II. I think I am a reincarnated pilot who was shot down the day I was born," Bill said with a New York accent.

I thought hard to figure out what the hell he was talking about and realized he was talking about reincarnation.

Bill taught school, sold encyclopedias, got multiple psychology degrees, a real estate license, and ran a massively successful career advisory business. He had no problem talking. A lot.

"How did you get involved in Osho's commune in Oregon?" I asked, hoping to get to the cult part. I wanted to know about the debauchery, mayhem, and free love. If anybody had an angle on love, it had to be thousands of hippies living in a commune with open sex and dance parties. Plus, he had been talking about his life resume for an hour, and I was about to fall asleep.

"I had a business partner ask me if I wanted to go to Oregon and hang out at a summer celebration and party for a week and make love," he responded nonchalantly. Now we were getting somewhere.

"I thought those people were crazy, but I was burned out from work and wanted a break for a week, so I agreed to go. I had seen those people at the Woodstock festival the year before. I thought they were nuts." Bill kept his perfect posture. Of course.

"Why did you stay?" I wondered what prompted him to stay the entire summer away from his real life and businesses.

"It was amazing. I am not going to say exactly what happened—" he smirked—"but there was a lot of free love, if you know what I mean. Why would I leave?"

Well, maybe because you were living in a cult that was about to implode, murder people, and allegedly kill its leader, I said silently to myself.

A blonde woman walked into the room. I had no idea there was another person in the apartment. Maybe she was a ghost. If so, she was an attractive ghost...fit, blonde, and younger than Bill.

"This is Sarah." He smiled while introducing her.

"How did you guys meet?" I asked as I started packing up my recorder. Hearing Bill talk about his summer at the cult was cool but didn't give me much direction on love. A bunch of hippies on drugs having sex. Free love. Controversy. No breakthroughs about finding love or being good at love, which was my real curiosity.

"I manifested her into my life," Bill said matter-of-factly, as if that was the only way to find a partner. I pulled my recorder back out.

"What?" I sat back down.

"I created the list of thirty-six," he said casually, looking at Sarah.

"What is the list of thirty-six?" I looked at Sarah too.

"If you want to meet someone, you create a list of thirty-six attributes you want in your perfect match. Then you imagine that person lying in your arms every night when you go to bed. Shortly after, they will walk into your life."

Come on, Bill. What Kool-Aid have you been drinking? It can't be that simple. I somewhat believe in manifesting, but this was a stretch.

"Really?" I looked back at Bill scratching my head.

He explained the system. He told me there are four categories with six requirements each. You take this structure and write down exactly what you want in a partner. The four categories are:

1. Physical attributes.

2. Educational requirements.

3. Religious affiliation and values.

4. Hobbies and interests.

He told me he made his own list that partly included a woman who was blonde, five-foot-six-inches tall, physically fit, enjoyed music, and liked flying. Sarah was all of those things.

"She matched thirty-three on my list of thirty-six," he said proudly.

After my meeting with Bill, I kept talking to people who had found the person of their dreams after deciding exactly what they wanted in a partner. They wrote it down. It made sense to me. It reminded me of people saying they wanted to be rich but not knowing exactly how rich. Or people wanting a car but not knowing what kind of car. We have to be crystal clear about what we want.

I am no manifesting guru, but I think there is something magical about deciding exactly who you want in your life and then visualizing them daily. Then your brain, the universe, God, Tom Cruise, or whatever you believe in will bring that perfect match right into your life. Does it make sense? Of course not. But just do it.

Speaking of that, my perfect girl is an Australian flight attendant and yoga instructor who is five-foot-five-inches tall, tan, with blue eyes and a free spirit. COME ON UNIVERSE... do your thing!

LOVE LESSONS

1. To find a partner, make your list of thirty-six characteristics you want them to have and visualize them in your arms at night as you go to sleep. Write down the thirty-six things you would love in your future partner and watch him or her walk into your life.

2. Perfect posture increases confidence, which attracts people to you. Become obsessed with your posture as you sit and stand; shoulders back, chin up, arms to the side. Your body language will draw people to you.

3. Join a cult if you want to have some fun for a summer!

30

THE SEX GODDESS

———

"Love is weird and yucky but everywhere, just like bananas."

GAVIN, FIVE YEARS OLD

"You can really have thirty-five orgasms in a row?" I avoided eye contact.

"Twenty-five," she corrected me. Whoops. Off by 40 percent. Tulum, Mexico, attracts these kinds of people. Free spirited, yoga-ish, energy-healing, crystal ball-holding wanders and self-proclaimed mystics. It has become a bohemian tourist town nestled along blazing white beaches in Southeastern Mexico. I was living there for a month when I heard rumors about a gal who teaches sex courses and claims to have thirty-five orgasms in a row. Sorry, twenty-five. Too much algebra.

Love was OBVIOUSLY in her wheelhouse. I had to find her.

She agreed to meet my friend Ilene and me to chat about love. I also brought my buddy Jake. He was coming off a three-day bender where he literally bought a flight from Atlanta the night before at 11:00 p.m. as he partied at a gay bar. He's not gay. It was his birthday. He is my hero.

We met the sex goddess at one of those super swanky beach hotels loaded with palm trees and fancy bedding. The kind of place that sells twenty-four-dollar drinks. I found out she ran their wellness programs, which included a sexuality course, and I begged Ilene to set up a meeting.

We arrived and wandered through the labyrinth of palm trees to the main beach area. She was sitting at a table alone, working on her laptop computer. A tiny lady, middle-aged, in a long, whimsical, bohemian outfit—no bra, flowing brown hair, and an oversized, flowing dress that showed off her body. That's how I imagine bohemian things, long and flowing.

She didn't seem nervous, but she did seem a little skeptical. I was nervous as usual, and sweating from the unrelenting heat and humidity. You could cut the air with a butter knife.

We settled into a quiet area of an outdoor bar. A bohemian bar. I sat on an awkward poof next to her. Ilene and Jake sat across the table from us on a bench with way too many oversized pillows. The mosquitos found my legs immediately.

I racked my brain for a question to start with other than "can you really have thirty-five, sorry, twenty-five orgasms in a row?" She sat confidently, waiting. Jake was turning green. Ilene adjusted the awkward pillows.

I have heard of women having a medical disorder called persistent genital arousal disorder (PGAD) that causes them to have a hundred orgasms a day.[29] My best friend is a doctor and told me he treats women with this disorder by injecting a nerve blocker into the area responsible for orgasms. He said it is like Botox for orgasms. Injecting anything into the orgasm area sounds about as fun as getting an eyeball tattoo.

---

29 Vanessa Chalmers, "Condition That Causes Women to Have up to 100 Orgasms a Day 'Could Be Caused by Damage to Nerves in the Spine That Control Sexual Arousal," Daily Mail, January 10, 2020.

The Sex Goddess, who goes by Bibi, was born in Poland and got a scholarship to a college in Milan, Italy. Since, she has moved all over the world. At one point, she had a midlife crisis and quit the corporate rat race and shifted into the wellness world.

She adjusted her long, flowing caftan and explained, "I am the wellness director of the hotel. I am also a conscious sexuality teacher, and I have a course called 'Energetic Lovemaking.'"

Sounded like a spaceship to me.

"So you are running the wellness program here and helping people figure out sex?" I slowly leaned over to scratch my legs without losing eye contact. The mosquitoes were going ballistic.

"Yeah, yeah!" Her voice grew louder as she smiled at the group.

I could tell she was comfortable in her own skin. She sat near me with her body open and unguarded. She wasn't overthinking the questions or offering canned answers. She'd pause after each question, looking up to think.

"What's the trick?" I shot a glance at Ilene and Jake.

She sighed. "I would say that instead of just having limited friction and goal-oriented, reproductive sex, we can tap into our sexuality, and that can energize and expand your consciousness. Connecting with a partner on a soul level really helps you to transcend to self-realization."

None of that made sense to me so I turned and asked Jake, "Do you talk during sex?"

"No." He said motionless. He was sweating out the past three days and hanging on by a thread. Jake is a tall and skinny rock star. He is the lead singer of his own band—Jacob and the Good People—and loves life. However, he was fourteen minutes away from dying of a hangover. Poor guy.

I looked at Bibi, seeing if she might tackle the question.

"Me? Not as much as I would like to. However, I think it starts there. Most of the couples I coach say no. Sex and silence." She laughed. "No one even knows how to start a conversation anymore."

I have heard communication is the key to hot, passionate, amazing sex. I suppose if we cannot communicate what we want during sex, how good can it be? I am a failure at communication in general. People-pleasing, fear, insecurity, and the walls I have built over time keep me shut down. I am jealous of people who fearlessly ask for what they want, like sending back food at restaurants because they don't like it.

"How do we have good sex?" I looked back to Bibi.

"It is really about coming into your body and senses, being present in your body and every sensation in your body. It is about dropping in and showing up rather than waiting and overthinking."

So far, I had learned communication and feeling the sensations in your body are the keys to good sex. I decided I would try it the next time I was fortunate enough to have sex. I had been on a solid dry spell for months and talking about sex with a sex coach was not helping. Jake stared into space. Ilene sat patiently, waiting to sneak in a few of her own questions.

Eventually, I asked the first question I always ask everybody.

"What is your definition of love?"

She thought for a moment, then said, "For me, it is the feeling of your heart being open. For me, love is an internal feeling." She further explained it starts inside us. It is about showing up. It is a decision and an action. "It's almost like I choose to show up, and I choose to listen."

"How do we do it?" I looked down at my legs to see if they were still there or if the mosquitos completely ate them.

"Yeah, it is like if I choose to take a course so I can communicate better, or I choose to commit to our weekly lovemaking practice. Even if I am tired, I commit to showing up. So it's really our everyday actions," she patiently explained.

I moved on to the second question I have asked everyone. "How many times have you been in love?"

"More than twenty I would say," she responded after a short pause. "The last person I fell in love with was actually myself. And through my journey over the past few years, I legitimately fell in love with myself," she said proudly. Honestly. Thankfully.

I was trying to get to the twenty-five orgasms question when she told us how she teaches women how to make love to themselves.

"I used to call it high vibrational masturbation," she laughed. Hmm. Should I ask her to teach me? Maybe a bad idea during this interview, I thought.

"I think we should learn how to make love to ourselves to grow self-love. I can make love to myself for two hours. I am sure you saw on my website that I can have twenty-five orgasms with or without a partner?" Her eyebrows raised.

Yes. Of course, I did. Why did she think we are here? "Yes, I think we came across that," I stammered.

I was starting to become attracted to her. Maybe it was all the sex talk? She had a confidence and such ease in the conversation, which was intriguing to me. I may or may not have imagined having sex with her. I may or may not have imagined her destroying me, like an insect eating the head off its mate after sex.

She never told me how she learned to have so many orgasms. She did, however, offer some interesting advice on how to love ourselves. "There are a couple of simple practices that one can do, okay?"

"Sure, go ahead," I replied, curious what she might offer since her journey to self-love sounded like a long one.

First, she said to make a recording of yourself on your cell phone. You make it really long, around ten minutes, and say all the things you love about yourself, such as:

- I love how fit I am.

- I love my eyes.

- I love how persistent I am in life.

- I love how radiant I am.

- I love how I never give up.

She said it might be hard at first, but the act of getting outside of your comfort zone was part of the process. Then you listen to the message daily so it gets burned into your subconscious.

She continued. "Another way to wire the messages into your brain is to listen to the message while you are pleasuring yourself. This ties the message, feeling, and belief together in the subconscious."

Maybe that one is better for women, I thought. I was not sure if I could listen to my dumbass say I love myself while I masturbated, but what did I know?

The second practice she mentioned was how she celebrated herself on a daily basis.

"Dressing up is a way of expressing myself. I love to create some creative, funky outfits. I love to get dressed up and take myself on a date. It is such a crazy thing to do. And one of my favorite things." She smiled warmly.

"Are you dating anyone?" I tried not to sound too creepy.

"No, that is a challenging area for me right now," she sighed. "You would think I of all people would have that figured out!"

Yes, I would think that.

I was impressed with her vulnerability and authenticity. She didn't hide behind the fact she was a human being like the rest of us and was having trouble dating, even though she was a love coach. She paused at one point and told me she realized she had to take action and go on dates if she wanted to find a partner. Something she had been avoiding. Something we all avoid at times.

"What is one question you would like to ask me?" I asked at the end of our time together, hoping Jake wouldn't pass out at the table.

"What is the number one thing you took away from this whole project?" she asked, referring to my journey around the world, looking for answers to love, and writing a book.

Interesting. I had never been asked that question before. Hell, I had never thought about that question before. I sat for a moment and really thought about what I had learned during the process. Then it was crystal clear.

"Connection. Connection is the most important thing in the world," I said, realizing that was the answer to everything from self-love, to romantic love, to love in general.

"Mic drop!" She laughed.

LOVE LESSONS

1. To fully engage sexually, we must connect with our bodies in the present moment and fully feel all the sensations. We must get out of our heads and into our bodies. We must also clearly communicate our desires and dislikes.

2. The journey to self-love and self-realization is a long, lonely road sometimes. However, it is okay to be alone during a season of life. That is when we find out who we are and come out a better person for others. In this season, we must practice self-love actions, from celebrating our wins internally to dressing up in funky outfits that make us feel good about ourselves and going on dates with ourselves alone.

3. The only way to reach twenty-five orgasms in a row is to reach twenty-four first.

31

THREE LOVE ANGELS

"Love is bananas because you can always find it if you just look."

– HANNAH, TWELVE YEARS OLD

Listen up, folks, this is a doozy. A full-blown journey into the world of the woo-woo. The unexplainable. Spirits and such. A bizarre story about the supernatural, love, and three ladies who entered my life one night.

I enrolled in a program to get certified as a life coach and attended a two-day intensive in Austin to fulfill program requirements. Ilene was also in the program, so we rented a two-bedroom Airbnb for the weekend. That is where it happened.

We arrived on Friday and had a long day of training on Saturday. I was packing up to leave when I overheard our two instructors talking about dreams. I perked up. Finally, a conversation about something other than coaching. We had been practicing coaching for hours.

"If you have a problem you can't figure out, try this…" one instructor said to a few of the students gathered around him.

He was an oddball. A soft-spoken, perfect posture, turtle-neck-shirt-tucked-into-tight-pants-wearing kind of guy. He talked in a hushed voice most of the time and sat quietly in meditation during breaks. The other instructor was unique with purple hair and jeans tucked into rhinestone cowboy boots. Welcome to Texas.

I moved closer to the group to hear the conversation.

Turtleneck continued his thought. "If you have a problem or something you can't figure out, try this...right before you go to bed tonight, set your journal beside your bed and leave it open to a blank page. Place a pen on top of the page. Next, right before you fall asleep, call on your dream angels and ask them the question you can't figure out. Then go to sleep. When you wake up, immediately turn over and start writing before your brain turns on. They will give you the answer nine times out of ten," he said with a gentle smile. I had to lean in because he talked so damn soft.

Hmm, I thought. I have dreams. I had a journal. I could find a pen. I was pretty much born for this.

"That is complete bullshit." Ilene glared at me as we left the training and walked to find some tequila and tacos. She is a rebel at heart. She also thinks all things woo-woo are garbage. "I never dream in the first place." She laughed at the idea of talking to my dream angels.

We grabbed some tequila and food, and headed back to the Airbnb. I kept talking about the dream angels, and she kept making fun of me. Pretty standard. She is the voice of reason, and I am Willy Wonka.

"I bet your dream angels come to you, and mine don't come to me!" I shot at her, heading to my room when we got back. She rolled her eyes and closed her door.

I set up my journal next to my bed as directed with a pen. I thought for a moment about how to word my question for the dream angels. Finally, in my mind, I said the following prayer: "Dream Angels, please come to me tonight and tell me why I have such a hard time with love. How do I love?"

I will be honest; it was weird talking to angels in your mind for the first time. Try it. Close your eyes and talk to angels right now. Weird, right?

I have dreams most nights. Oddly, since my father died when I was twenty-one, he has only appeared in two of my dreams. He appeared in one shortly after he died, in which he told me everything was okay, and I woke up hysterical. The second time was a year later where he just looked at me from afar. I believe he was communicating with me from the "other side" both times. Very powerful. Very emotional. Both times I woke up crying like a seven-year-old girl.

I went to bed excited for the next morning.

I woke up around 7:00 a.m. and immediately turned and wrote. After a few sentences, I stopped and read what I wrote. The word love appeared a few times, but the rest was gobbledygook. Very lackluster. I kept trying to find a hidden message in the words, but nothing seemed important, interesting, or coherent. Must be a hoax.

Defeated, I wandered into the kitchen to grab some water. Ilene came out of her room a few minutes later and asked me how it went with the dream angels.

"Well, I am not sure. Maybe, maybe not," I said, thinking back to the nonsense I wrote in my journal.

"You are not going to believe what happened to me," she clasp her hands together in excitement.

"What?" I stopped and looked at her.

"I had a crazy dream last night where these three love angels came to me. They looked like old women. It was crazy!" She raised her arms. "They were laughing. Then they said to me, 'Tell him all he has to do is love, it's already in him. He just makes it hard.' And they laughed like it was so silly you think you don't know how to love!"

A bolt of energy shot through my body. I immediately knew exactly what they were trying to tell me. It all made sense to me. Love is easy. It is right in front of me. All I have to do is open my eyes. Just love. I still get chills thinking about that moment.

Since, I have made it a practice to call on my three love angels when I am upset, confused, or in need of help. I call on them for advice, answers, and just for fun sometimes. I can see them smiling and laughing in my mind. I can see them look at me as if everything is going to be okay. I guess I am nuts.

However, they are always near and ready when I need them.

The other day, I was struggling to figure out where to look for my research for this book. It was a Sunday morning, and I was leaving a hipster coffee shop to walk back to my loft. So for fun, I called on my love angels and asked them to give me a sign or show me where to look for some research. Then I opened up podcasts on iTunes on my phone, and the first thing that popped up was a podcast I had never seen before called *This is Love*. It was a story about a swimmer reuniting a baby whale with its mother. The story blew me away and was an amazing story of love.

I am not sure what is on the other side, or if there are spirits among us. I can't explain the unexplainable. However, my dad comes to me sometimes, as do my love angels. I am grateful for both of them. They help make life a little easier.

If you are having a hard time, call on your dream angels. Tell them you are struggling and need help. Let them give you answers in your dreams. Look for signs, believe in miracles. They are all around you.

LOVE LESSONS

1. If you look for the signs, they are there. If you believe in angels, they are there. Ask for help and be open to the answers. Say prayers of gratitude to your angels or passed relatives. Lean on them for help.

2. When calling on your angels, ask for a sign. Tell them you want a sign to appear in the next twenty-four hours to guide you. Then keep your eyes open.

3. Love is not that complicated. It is everywhere if we just open our eyes and believe.

32

THE LAST LETTER

—

Dear Trey,

I love you. I really do. It has been a long, hard road, and here we are. I am proud of you. Proud because life is not easy and you keep showing up. I am proud of you for writing this book and for all the hell you went through to do it. I am proud of you for being a kind person. A light burns inside of you brighter than the sun. Let it shine.

I love you because even though you slip sometimes, you get back up. I love you because you are hilarious and sexy. I love you because you are one in seven billion.

Keep living out loud. Keep chasing the stars and dancing on the moon. Remember your purpose, to help the person in front of you.

Keep pushing, creating, laughing, and loving. Be kind to yourself. Always be kind to yourself.

Remember, you are easy to love.

I love you.

Trey

9/7/20

Montego Bay, Jamaica

33

IN THE END

Mr. Rogers once said, "Frankly, there isn't anyone you couldn't learn to love once you've heard their story."[30] I agree. Stories connect us, inspire us, and teach us. When we hear each other's stories, we find we are all the same. I hope the stories in this book have touched your heart. I hope you have laughed, cried, and thought I am a complete lunatic at times. I love you, and I mean it.

In the end, life is about connection. That's it. Pure and simple. Ring the bell. Full stop. I'm a guru.

Connection with ourselves and with others. Connection to a life of adventure. Connection to something greater than us. The essentials. I think love is always right in front of us if we just open our eyes.

It is inside us when we realize we are enough and worthy. It is in the magical moments of adventure, from having coffee with a friend to jumping off a cliff in Jamaica. It is in the first kiss, the arms of a lover, or looking into your child's eyes for the first time.

---

30   Diana Bruk, "12 Beautiful Life Lessons Mr. Rogers Taught Us," Good Housekeeping, December 5, 2014.

Love, that crazy, undefinable, radical, zany, lopsided, magical and mystical wonder of the world, is simply connection. And, for the record, it is all that matters.

As I was writing this book (and suffering massive panic attacks as my editors kept pumping me full of affirmations), people kept asking me why bananas. Why is love bananas?

I was twenty-two years old the first time I traveled overseas. My friend Billy and I spent three months backpacking through Central America. We walked, bused, and trained from the Panama Canal to the Texas border. Every morning I would eat a banana from a roadside vendor or cafe. No matter where I was, I always found plenty of bananas. Since, as I have traveled to over one hundred countries, I have never been anywhere that didn't have bananas for sale. They are available everywhere, around the world. Just like love.

Bananas are also yellow, the happiest color in the world. They are fun and playful. They are sweet and delicious and come in the perfect wrapping. Just like us.

Bananas start green, grow into a magnificent yellow, and finally suffer a few bruises and spots as they age. Just like us.

Finally, bananas grow together in a bunch. Just like us. We only grow when we are together.

I hope you find love and bananas everywhere you look. I hope every time you see a banana it reminds you to focus on love and remember you are love.

Finally, I have one last request of you. It is the most important part of this entire book. If there is only one takeaway from all these pages, please make it this one...

Write three love letters.

The first one should be to yourself. This is the most important one. Without you, there is no *them*. Handwrite the letter.

Second, write to the one person in your life who needs to hear from you the most right now. You know who it is. Write it. Mail it.

The third needs to go to your partner—your ride-or-die, the love of your life, the most important person in the world. And if you don't have one yet, write to her or him so when you do meet, the letter has already been written. Leave it under the pillow.

Love,

Trey

ACKNOWLEDGMENTS

The hardest part was starting. The second hardest part was getting people to believe in me. I am blessed to have these folks in my life, and through their support, this book became a reality. Grateful is a bastardized word these days, but I am unbelievably grateful for you.

Thanks, Mom. Can you believe we made it this far? Your support and belief in me are the only reasons I have ever achieved anything. I Love you!

Thank you to my two editors, Cassandra Caswell and Carol McKibben, who kept me from jumping off of a cliff and quitting a thousand times.

Thanks to Ilene Rosh, who not only secured all of my interviews, but has edited all of my writings over the past few years. You are the FROL!

And thank you to everyone who gave me their time for a personal interview; pre-ordered the eBook, paperback, and multiple copies to make publishing possible; helped spread the word about *Love is Bananas* to gather amazing momentum; and helped me publish a book I am proud of. You are amazing and I can't wait to read your books!

Adam Meadows

Adam Tedder

Ahsan Shah

Aleesa C. Daley

Alexander Barclay

Ali Bowers

Allison Price

Allison R Stephens

Allyson Greenfield

Alvin D Moore, Jr.

Andrea Coonrod

Andrew Averso

Andrew Nitsch

Angie Coonrod

April & Andy McKoski

April Pitman

Ashley David

Ashley Patrick

Ben Rasnick

Benny Murray

Bert Maes

Bill Thaxton

Blythe Fisher

Brent Hesse

Brett Belcastro

Bridgett Rich

Britney Kelly

Chad "Fat Dave" Stephens

Chuck Barnwell

Corey Jacobs

Craig Tilley

Crystal Lewis

David Broughton

David Lyons

David Rogers

Dawn Evans

Deanna Amodeo

Diana Hardy

Emily Lipman

Emyrald Sinclaire

Eric De Steeg

Eric Koester

Gaela Peters

Garrett Dodson

George Davis

Greg Horner

Greg Wood

Gyl Grinberg

Hadley Moore

Haneen Iahseh

Hannah Collier

Holly Waltman

Jason Bussey

Ivy Smith

Jackie Hornsby

Jackie Hovarth

Jacob Blazer

James Labrot

Jamey Shirah

Jamie Greiver

Jamie Konn

Jamie L. Patterson

Jason Jones

Jeff "Boss" Corban

Jeff Croft

Jeff Danielly

Jennifer Cunningham

Jennifer Leibowitz

Jennifer Lingvall

Jennifer Wagner

Jenny Holding

Jeremy Hamff

Jessica Bencina

Jessica Christenson

Jessica Collins

Jessica Mogill

Jessica Reece Fagan

Jill Vincenzi

Johnny Liu

Jonathan Sheer

Jose Marin

Joseph Bowers

Josh Feingold

Josh Miller

Judy Humphreys

Julie Secrist

Justin Ehrecke

Katia Fulks

Kelley Knight

Kelli Meyer

Kelsety Metz

Keri New

Kevin R. Fisher

Kim Fong

Kim Pugh

Kristin Howard &
Alex Stimson

Kristin McNitt

Kristina Graham

Kristine K. Carder

Kyle Goodrich

Lacy Dicharry

Laura Diem

Laura Lee Henson

Lauren Moret

Lee Blankenship

Louis Raffaele

Lyndsey Wheat

Maggie Urrutia

Mandi Oeland

Marissa Stephens

Mary Strange

Matthew Nielson

Meagan Jain

Meg Allwein

Meg Day

Melanie Wilson

Melissa J. Harris

Melissa Love Kennedy

Melissa Zatzkis

Meryl Rindsberg

Michael K. O'Kelly

Michael Zeise

Michele Brown

Michelle Rossi

Mike Barnhill

Mike Feldberg

Mike Mashke

Mitali Chakraborty

Molly Darby

Monique Evans

Ned Mason

Nick Tapp

Paige Welch

Papa Sean

Pat Barton

Patty Gorman

Renee Nagy

Robb Lejuwaan

Robroy Wiley

Sara Fort

Scott "Ski" Feinstein

Shae Parker

Shanie Alpert Spencer

Stacy O'Kelley

Stephen Neslage

Suzanne Clark

Tabitha Patch

Ted Haynes

Teddy Gillen

Thomas Bell

Thomas Howard

Tim Carlson

Tina Yates

Tobie McElrath

Trey Mock

Tribble Reese

Wade Galt

William McLane

Zachary Gatch

APPENDIX

———

MY FAKE FATHER

"Gestalt Therapy." Psychology Today. Accessed August 10, 2020.
https://www.psychologytoday.com/us/therapy-types/gestalt-therapy.

Hoyt, Alia. "Why Do We Fall in Love?" How Stuff Works. February 8, 2018.
https://health.howstuffworks.com/relationships/love/why-do-we-fall-in-love.htm.

JOLLY MEETS MOTORMOUTH

Appalachian Trail Conservancy. "The Adventure of a Lifetime: Thru-Hiking."
Accessed July 15, 2020.
https://appalachiantrail.org/explore/hike-the-a-t/thru-hiking/.

JUST DO IT

Brown, Brene. *The Gifts of Imperfection: Let Go of Who You Think You're Supposed to
Be and Embrace Who You Are.* Center City, Hazel, 2010.

Kessler, Martin, ed. WBUR (blog).
https://www.wbur.org/onlyagame/2018/11/23/just-do-it-nike-gilmore.

THE MONKS HANDS

Goalcast. "Top 20 Most Inspiring Dalai Lama Quotes." Accessed September 12, 2020.
https://www.goalcast.com/2017/03/09/top-20-most-inspiring-dalai-lama-quotes/.

FRANK'S LOVE LETTER

Sinatra, Nancy. *Legend: Frank Sinatra and the American Dream.* Santa Monica:
General Publishing Group, 1998.

PREACHERS AND POISON: PART 1

Wilking, Spencer, and Lauren Effron, "Snake-Handling Pentecostal Pastor Dies
from Snake Bite." ABC News. February 17, 2014.
https://abcnews.go.com/US/snake-handling-pentecostal-pastor-dies-snake-bite/
story?id=22551754.

HUGS IN BALI

Cirino, Erica. "What Are the Benefits of Hugging." Healthline. April 10, 2018. https://www.healthline.com/health/hugging-benefits#1.-Hugs-reduce-stress-by-showing-your-support.

Pew Research Center. "The Future of World Religions: Population Growth Projections, 2010-2050." Last modified April 2, 2015. http://www.globalreligiousfutures.org/countries/indonesia#/?affiliations_religion_id=0&affiliations_year=2010&region_name=All%20Countries&restrictions_year=2016.

THE TERRIFYING TEA

Leonard, Jayne. "What to know about ayahuasca." Medical News Today. January 31, 2020. Accessed April 23, 2020. https://www.medicalnewstoday.com/articles/ayahuasca#how-does-it-work.

DYING FOR SEX

Boyer, Nikki. "Becoming Whole." March 11, 2020. In *Dying for Sex*. Produced by Wondery. Podcast, MP3 audio. 48:13. https://wondery.com/shows/dying-for-sex/.

Roll, Rich. "The Best Monologue EVER: Zach Bush, MD | Rich Roll Podcast." Jan 9, 2019, video, 4:28. https://www.youtube.com/watch?v=aLaVutWXju0&t=16s.

TWO BEST FRIENDS

Equal Justice Initiative. "Anthony Ray Hinton." Accessed September 19, 2020. https://eji.org/cases/anthony-ray-hinton/.

"Oprah Winfrey Facebook Live with Anthony Ray Hinton." June 28, 2018, YouTube Video, 31:12. https://www.youtube.com/watch?v=T_fr8huY3yo&t=301s.

Winfrey, Oprah, and Anthony Ray Hinton. "EP.#102: Anthony Ray Hinton, Part 1: Freedom After 30 Years on Death Row." January 5, 2019. In Super Soul Podcast. Produced by Harpo Studios. YouTube Video. https://www.youtube.com/watch?v=GSrj4oQjJxE.

Winfrey, Oprah, and Anthony Ray Hinton. "EP. #103: Anthony Ray Hinton, Part 2: Finding LIfe, Hope and Redemption on Death Row." January 6, 2019. In Super Soul Podcast. Produced by Harpo Studios. YouTube Video. https://www.youtube.com/watch?v=GSrj4oQjJxE.

BOB'S LOVE LETTER

Dorlita, J. "Bob Marley Quote on Love." *Private Love Letters* (blog). January 23, 2013. https://privateloveletters.wordpress.com/2013/01/23/bob-marley-quote-on-love/.

THIRTY SIX THINGS

Wolfson, Sam. "The Free-Love Cult that Terrorized America—and Became Netflix's Latest Must-Watch." *The Guardian*, April 7, 2018. US Edition. https://www.theguardian.com/tv-and-radio/2018/apr/07/cult-oregon-1980s-terror-netflix-documentary-..

THE SEX GODDESS

Chalmers, Vanessa. "Condition That Causes Women to Have up to 100 Orgasms a Day 'Could Be Caused by Damage to Nerves in the Spine That Control Sexual Arousal.'" *Daily Mail*, January 10, 2020.
https://www.dailymail.co.uk/health/article-7873057/Condition-causes-100-ORGASMS-day-caused-lesions-nerves-spine.html.

THE END

Bruk, Diana. "12 Beautiful Life Lessons Mr. Rogers Taught Us." *Good Housekeeping*, December 5, 2014.
https://www.goodhousekeeping.com/life/inspirational-stories/a22776/life-lessons-mrrogers/.